PRE-HSE

Core Skills in Reading & Writing

New Readers Press®
ProLiteracy's publishing division

Photos courtesy of:

p. 33: © Igor Bulgarin; p. 35: © rck_953; p. 37: © photobyphotoboy; p. 38: © artybloke; p. 48: © Katrina Brown; p. 51: © Comstock; p. 55: © David Henderson; p. 66: © Fotosr52; p. 79: © Thomas Northcut; p. 84: © Monkey Business Images; p. 90: © Fotokostic; p. 96: OLJ Studio; p. 115: © chrisdomey; p. 121: © Russell Shively

Pre-HSE Core Skills in Reading and Writing
ISBN 978-1-56420-882-8

Proceeds from the sale of New Readers Press materials support professional development, training, and technical assistance programs of ProLiteracy that benefit local literacy programs in the U.S. and around the globe.

Developer: QuaraCORE
Editorial Director: Terrie Lipke
Cover Design: Carolyn Wallace
Technology Specialist: Maryellen Casey

CONTENTS

CONTENTS

Welcome to *Core Skills in Reading and Writing*, an important resource in helping you build a solid foundation of reading, writing, and English language skills as you gear up to start preparing for the GED®, TASC, or HiSET® high school equivalency Reading and Writing test.

How to Use This Book

Pretest

The first step in using *Core Skills in Reading and Writing* is to take the Pretest, which begins on the next page. This test will show which skills you already have and which areas you need to practice. After taking the Pretest and checking your answers, use the chart on page 11 to find the lessons that will help you study the skills you need to improve.

Reading and Writing Skills Lessons

The book is organized into six units, each containing brief lessons that focus on specific skills. Units 1–3 cover reading skills for literature and informational texts; Unit 4 focuses on language and grammar; and Units 5 and 6 provide instruction on writing. Read each of the lessons, which also include tips to help you understand skills and concepts:

- Real-World Connections describe how reading and writing concepts connect to our everyday lives.
- Skills Tips offer clues for easy ways to remember rules and skills discussed in the lessons.
- Vocabulary Tips provide additional examples and other advice on using and remembering key terms.

Important vocabulary terms are listed under Key Terms on the first page of each lesson. These words appear in **boldface** when they are first used in each lesson. You can use the Glossary at the end of the book to look up definitions of key terms.

Each lesson ends with a brief Lesson Review that includes questions to test your knowledge of the content that was covered. Answers can be found in the Answer Key, beginning on page 153.

Each unit concludes with a Unit Practice Test that covers all the content in the unit's lessons. In the Answer Key, you will find explanations to help your understanding with many Unit Test questions.

Posttest

After completing all the units, you can test what you know by taking the Posttest, beginning on page 142. This test will help you check your understanding of all the skills in the book. It will also help determine if you are ready to move on to high school equivalency test preparation.

Answer the following questions to test your knowledge of reading and writing content and skills.

1. What is the setting of a story?

   A. the author's birthplace

   B. the time and place a story takes place

   C. the movement of fictional characters from one location to another

   D. the length of time required for the story to take place

2. Which sentence is an example of a first-person narrator?

   A. Annie went to the office to speak to Tim.

   B. The whole community felt the need to volunteer.

   C. You were ready to go to work.

   D. I stopped at the door.

3. Which of the following is NOT a purpose of a minor character?

   A. to give the story atmosphere

   B. to move the plot forward

   C. to be central to the development of the plot

   D. to help describe other characters

4. Which of the following is NOT an example of external conflict?

   A. character against character

   B. character against his conscience

   C. character against nature

   D. character against society

Write your response on the line provided.

5. The hero or villain of a story is which type of character?

   _____

6. What do you call the series of related events that gives the story a beginning, middle, and ending?

   _____

Read the following passage, and then answer questions 7–9.

Myra's Birthday

Myra's birthday was always a festive occasion. Her family decorated the dining room with colorful balloons that bobbed about in the fan's breeze. Her mother made a moist chocolate cake. Her siblings sang the birthday song loudly as their mouths watered in anticipation of the cutting of the cake.

7. Identify at least three words or phrases in the passage that indicate mood.

   _____

   _____

   _____

8. What is the author's tone in the passage "Myra's Birthday"?

   _____

9. What is the subject of the passage "Myra's Birthday"?

   A. Myra and her family make celebrating birthdays a fun tradition.

   B. Myra enjoys the attention she gets on her birthday.

   C. Myra's siblings only care about eating the chocolate cake.

   D. Myra's family likes to decorate the dining room for holidays.

10. The subject of a work of literature is its

   A. plot structure.

   B. main topic.

   C. moral.

   D. theme.

Read the following poem, and then answer questions 11–16.

Summer Lullabies

An owl gazes up at the silvery moon,
Quietly whispering, "Who, who, who . . ."
Cicadas and tree frogs also sing,
They're weaving a song of shadowy things.

Silent as a shadow, the owl lifts her feathers,
Wings outspread, she conducts with pleasure
A summer symphony under shimmering light;
I close my eyes and whisper, "Good night."

11. Which literary device best describes the line "A summer symphony under shimmering light"?

   A. metaphor
   B. personification
   C. hyperbole
   D. onomatopoeia

12. The rhyme scheme of this verse is

   A. ABAB/CDCD.
   B. ABBA/CDDC.
   C. AABB/CCDD.
   D. ABCB/DEFE.

13. In the poem, the owl most likely symbolizes

   A. mystery.
   B. strange dreams.
   C. wisdom.
   D. creative leadership.

14. "Silent as a shadow" is an example of

   A. simile.
   B. rhyme.
   C. hyperbole.
   D. onomatopoeia.

15. What tone do the last four lines of the poem convey?

   A. forgiving
   B. protective
   C. energetic
   D. peaceful

16. How would you describe the speaker's feelings about night, nature, and dreams?

   _____

   _____

Read the following passage, and then answer questions 17–19.

Maria: Have you packed the truck for the trip? *(She briskly walks into the kitchen and looks at the empty cooler on the floor. She furrows her eyebrows as she sees JT eating a banana.)* We're supposed to leave in ten minutes, and we need lots of water and fresh fruit in the cooler. It's always so hot at the beach.

JT: No worries! I got it! I've been clearing out the truck. Besides, we have plenty of time.

Maria: You know I hate to be late. *(She opens the refrigerator and starts loading water bottles into the cooler.)*

JT: *(Calmly takes the bottles out of Maria's hands, places them in the cooler, and then whispers in her ear.)* Relax. You always get so nervous when we go to these family outings. *(Chuckles.)* Remember when you rushed out of the house during the holidays and you forgot to bring the pie? Why don't you put the beach towels in the truck, and I'll get this packed up! *(Winks and smiles at Maria.)*

17. Based on the stage directions and dialogue, what can you conclude about Maria's character?

   A. She is self-confident and flexible.
   B. She is anxious and particular.
   C. She likes to confront her problems.
   D. She loses her temper easily.

18. The dialogue between Maria and JT establishes

   A. the plot of the play.
   B. what the family outing is about.
   C. why Maria is nervous about the outing.
   D. the differences between the two characters.

19. Explain how the stage directions help reveal JT's character.

   _____

   _____

   _____

Read the following passage, and then answer questions 20–24.

At Your Service

Service animals are a common sight in today's world. You may see them guiding a visually impaired person across a busy street or aiding a person in a wheelchair. These invaluable animals help people with disabilities
[5] live independently. They can be trained to carry out many different tasks.

The idea of service animals is not new. People relied on their four-footed companions as far back as ancient Rome. By the eighteenth century—a more systematic training of
[10] dog breeds to help the visually impaired began. The more widespread use of dogs as service animals began in the early to mid-twentieth century.

Although dogs are the most widely used service animal, other animals have made their mark in this area.
[15] Miniature horses are used to guide the visually impaired. Animals used for emotional support include cats, rabbits, ferrets, some types of birds, and even pigs!

20. What is the main purpose of this passage?

   A. to inform the reader about service animals

   B. to convince the reader to use a service animal

   C. to summarize the history of service animals

   D. to entertain the reader with a story about a service animal

21. As it is used in paragraph 1 (line 4), the word *invaluable* most nearly means

   A. rare.   **C.** expensive.

   B. important.   **D.** distinctive.

Correct the punctuation error in the underlined portion of this sentence.

22. By the <u>eighteenth century—a more systematic</u> training of dog breeds to help the visually impaired began.

_____

_____

23. Write the main idea of the last paragraph on the lines provided.

_____

_____

24. How are service animals different from pets?

_____

_____

Rewrite the following sentence to correct the error in agreement.

25. Students who wished to go on the field trip to the capitol building should wait for the buses by the front entrance to the school.

_____

_____

_____

Combine the following sentences into one grammatically correct sentence.

26. Marco and Christina finished their project. They spent the rest of the afternoon at the park.

_____

_____

_____

Correct the capitalization error in this sentence.

27. We agreed to meet at Sombrero Beach, but traffic on Begonia street was so bad that we could not get through.

_____

_____

_____

28. What purpose does an adjective serve in a sentence?

_____

_____

Correct the spelling error in this sentence.

29. My teacher asked me to repeet the exercise until I felt comfortable moving on to the next lesson.

_____

_____

Identify whether the purpose of each of the following writing prompts is expository or persuasive.

30. Describe why you should be given a scholarship to study abroad.

_____

31. Write a presentation for your colleagues explaining how to use the new security system.

_____

32. Write a letter to the editor of your local newspaper explaining why a change in the local recycling rules is a bad idea.

_____

Read the following passage, and then answer questions 33–38.

[1] The right to vote has always been an important part of American freedom. [2] But hand-in-hand with this freedom is another: the right *not* to vote. [3] Every election, large percentages of Americans do not cast their votes. [4] In a nation whose rights have been hard fought across centuries, the number of non-voters is unsettling. [5] Every eligible American should vote!

[6] Elected policymakers know who votes. [7] Voter turnout is recorded, along with data about voters. [8] In recent elections, 80 to 99 percent of wealthy citizens voted. [9] But for lower-income citizens, voter turnout was well under 70 percent. [10] As a result, politicians are less likely to cater to them. [11] If voter turnout were more equal, the elected officials would have concern for all groups.

[12] So few people vote these days that it's like we don't care that that makes us undemocratic. [13] Today's unbalanced voter turnout is strikingly inconsistent with our history of celebrating equal rights. [14] In democracy, representation matters more than many people realize. [15] Citizens' voices cannot be heard unless they are expressed. [16] Voting is the means of that expression.

33. Which phrase best describes the purpose of this essay?

    A. to persuade non-voters that they should vote

    B. to criticize politicians who ignore non-voters' needs

    C. to explain how the voting process works

    D. to argue that democracy includes the right not to vote

34. Which sentence in paragraph 2 is an example of supporting evidence?

    A. 6   **C.** 10

    B. 7   **D.** 11

35. Which makes the best topic sentence for paragraph 2?

    A. American voters are voting in historically low numbers.

    B. Wealthy people control the country through campaign contributions to political candidates.

    C. Voters not only affect election turnout by voting, but they also affect elected officials' priorities.

    D. Many voters argue that their votes should remain private, but sadly this is not the case.

36. Which sentence offers the best conclusion for paragraph 3?

    A. In America, every vote matters.

    B. Voting should be made mandatory so that every American voice is heard and heeded.

    C. There ought to be a better way to make our opinions known than every four years at the polls.

    D. If we do not reverse this trend, America will become the laughingstock of the world.

37. Which sentence from paragraph 2 contains a transition word or phrase?

    A. 7

    B. 8

    C. 9

    D. 10

38. How should sentence 12 be rewritten to give it a more formal tone?

    A. It'd be like we cared more if more people voted.

    B. It's mortifying the way other people must look at us these days, since so few people vote anymore.

    C. If we could be bothered to vote, we'd at least look more like we were a real democracy.

    D. Despite owning the right to vote, few voters currently exercise that right.

1. B.
2. D.
3. C.
4. B.
5. main
6. plot
7. Possible answers: festive, colorful, bobbed about, loudly, mouths watered, anticipation
8. The author's tone is happy.
9. A.
10. B.
11. A.
12. C.
13. D.
14. A.
15. D.
16. Possible answer: The speaker admires the beauty and wonderful sounds of nature. The sounds provide a soothing pathway to dreams and help the speaker fall asleep.
17. B.
18. D.
19. Possible answer: JT takes the water from Maria and starts loading the cooler. He whispers, smiles, winks at her, and chuckles. These actions reveal that JT is easy-going and is trying to get Maria in a good mood.
20. A.
21. B.
22. eighteenth century, a more systematic
23. Although dogs are the most widely used type of service animal, other animals have made their mark providing aid and assistance to people.
24. Service animals work to help people with disabilities live independently instead of simply providing companionship.
25. Students who **wish** to go on the field trip to the capitol building should wait for the buses by the front entrance to the school.

26. Marco and Christina finished their project, so they spent the rest of the afternoon at the park.
27. We agreed to meet at Sombrero Beach, but traffic on Begonia **Street** was so bad that we could not get through.
28. The purpose of an adjective is to describe a noun.
29. My teacher asked me to **repeat** the exercise until I felt comfortable moving on to the next lesson.
30. persuasive
31. expository
32. persuasive
33. A.
34. B.
35. C.
36. A.
37. D.
38. D.

Check your answers. Review the questions you did not answer correctly. You can use the chart below to locate lessons in this book that will help you learn more about reading and writing skills. Which lessons do you need to study? Work through the book, paying close attention to the lessons in which you missed the most questions. At the end of the book, you will have a chance to take another test to see how much your score improves.

Question	Where to Look for Help		
	Unit	Lesson	Page
1	1	1	13
2	1	2	15
3, 5, 9, 19	1	3	18
4, 6	1	4	21
7, 8, 38	1	5	25
10	1	6	28
11, 14	2	3	40
12	2	1	35
13	2	2	37
15, 16	2	4	44
17, 21	3	4	65
18	2	7	50
19	2	6	48
20, 23, 24, 34, 35	3	2	59
22	4	5	95
25	4	6	99
26	4	3	88
27	4	7	102
28	4	1	80
29	4	9	108
30, 31, 32, 33	3	5	68
36	3	4	65
37	5	3	121

Reading Fiction and Prose

You are in a harsh and barren environment. Around you is a strange, intimidating landscape filled with bizarre plants and creatures you have never seen before. You feel threatened and uncomfortable. A stranger approaches. Is he a friend or foe?

Reading fiction is more than just understanding what happens. It includes analyzing how a particular character, tone, and point of view, among other things, add to the story's meaning. This unit will help you learn to interpret the elements of fiction and increase your understanding and enjoyment of it.

The author's decision of where and when to set a story contributes to its overall meaning. This lesson will help you identify and interpret a story's setting.

Time and Place

Setting describes the time and location in which a story takes place. It can range as widely as an author's imagination—from present-day North America to an imaginary and long-ago universe with inhabitants wildly different from Earth's. When reading a story, the first element to assess is setting. *When* and *where* does the story take place?

Read this paragraph from a story:

> The two men left the city in the early morning, drove all day, and reached the shore of the southernmost lake at sunset. There they camped and sorted their packs, leaving in the truck anything too heavy to be given space. At sunrise, they decamped, loaded the canoe, and shoved off. The air was clearer than home, and everything was silent. The lake water was navy blue with the sky reflected in it. There were five portages before noon, varying from a comfortable 20 rods to a back-breaking 160 rods.

In order to assess the setting in a book or story, underline any words that offer you clues about it. Setting clues could include any of the following:

- technology [*Are the characters riding horses?*]
- speech [*Are the characters using old-fashioned language?*]
- geography [*Are the characters climbing a mountain?*]
- weather [*Is it snowing?*]
- any unusual elements [*Is it snowing cotton candy?*]

In this example, there is a truck, which tells us that the time is modern. There is a lake. So far, this story does not seem likely to take place in a highly fantastical, entirely made-up universe.

What about time? The story tells us directly that the time is between sunrise and noon.

This story seems likely to take place here and now—and, so far at least, it takes place in a fairly short time frame, not over decades or centuries.

Key Term

setting

Skills Tip

Look closely at the vocabulary used in a story in order to determine its setting. Are there many unfamiliar words? If so, consider the possibility that the text isn't just too difficult, but that the author is using specific vocabulary to let you know that the story is set somewhere unusual.

Complete the activities below to check your understanding of the lesson content. The Unit 1 Answer Key is on page 153.

Vocabulary

Write a definition in your own words for the key term.

1. setting _____

_____

Skills Practice

Read the paragraph carefully and answer the questions that follow.

The only way Commander Hurley could repair the oxygen module was with a compression tank. Hurley checked the logs; Station 4, on Cassini, had the last two tanks. Requesting a delivery pod would take weeks—that is, if the commander there granted Hurley's request. The Station 4 Commander, a Swede named Johansson, was a stalwart sycophant who played by the rules. He would grill Hurley about the accident that had knocked his module off-line. Hurley would have to swallow his pride and make the request. His crew was counting on him. In the meantime, they'd keep the drills running, and perhaps soon they'd strike a vein of mercury beneath the planet's barren crust to make the whole mission worthwhile.

2. In your own words, identify the setting of the story.

_____

_____

_____

3. Which details and words helped you to determine the story's setting?

_____

_____

_____

Every story is told from a point of view. A story's point of view affects how the reader identifies, or does not identify, with particular characters.

A story always emphasizes the experiences of one or more characters over those of others. One way this is done is by presenting the story from a particular **point of view**—the perspective of the person telling the story. This lesson will help you understand point of view.

First Person

A story told from the **first-person** point of view is told the way you would tell about something that happened to you. A **narrator** is the person who tells the story. A first-person narrator will say things such as, "And then I met Mr. Childers" and "I was nervous about the job interview."

Read the following paragraph from a short story:

> I took a deep breath and hurried along the dock, searching for my ride. Finally at the end of the dock, I spotted her—sleek, shiny, and built for speed. I took another deep breath and made my way aboard—today was my day; I could feel it. Today I was going to win the camp sailing trophy.

This story is happening to the person who is telling it. It includes the words "I" and "my."

A first-person narrator will describe the story's events from his or her own point of view. The narrator is a character in the story and as such will not know other characters' motivations or feelings.

Third Person

A story told from the **third-person** point of view is a story happening to somebody else. The narrator is not a character in the story and will not use the words "I" or "me." The two types of third-person point of view are limited and omniscient.

In a story told from the **third-person limited** point of view, the narrator can describe the thoughts of *only one* particular character. Read the following paragraphs:

> "Glad you could join us, Master Stewart," replied Professor Tompkins.
>
> Henry suspected Tompkins probably was glad—but not because he had come to class. Henry watched as the teacher's face cracked into what passed for a grin—at least for Tompkins—and quickly took his seat. Henry was willing to bet that his tardiness might have been the highpoint of Tompkins' day.

This narrator is describing events that are happening to two people: Henry and Professor Tompkins.

Key Terms

first-person

narrator

point of view

third-person

third-person limited

third-person omniscient

Skills Tip

As a reader, your perspective may be different from that of the characters—even the main character. If the point of view is limited, you may know even more than the main character does about certain things.

However, Henry, not Tompkins, feels like the main character. Why is that? Certain words give you clues about Henry's thoughts and feelings: "Henry suspected," "Henry was willing to bet." The only way the narrator can know this is by having access to Henry's mind.

This story is told from a third-person limited point of view because the narrator is limited in what he or she can describe—in this case, the thoughts and feelings of Henry, but not those of Tompkins.

Omniscient or Limited?

Omniscient (ahm-NIH-shunt) means "all-knowing." In a **third-person omniscient** story, the narrator is telling somebody else's story but has access to multiple characters' thoughts and feelings. Read the following paragraph:

> By the time the summer sun peeked over the new bank building, the hitching posts had started to fill up, and conversation began to be heard. Ranchers came in for supplies, and there was a new teacher named Miss Gileston, who rode a fussy brown mare and took her breakfast at the café before greeting the children at the door of the schoolhouse. Townspeople thought that daily breakfast in a café ought to be beyond the means of a schoolteacher's meager salary, and they regarded Miss Gileston suspiciously.

In this story, the narrator knows how the townspeople in general feel about Miss Gileston. This is a third-person omniscient point of view.

Complete the activities below to check your understanding of the lesson content. The Unit 1 Answer Key is on page 153.

Vocabulary

Write definitions in your own words for each of the key terms.

1. point of view _____
   _____

2. first-person _____
   _____

3. third-person _____
   _____

4. third-person limited _____
   _____

5. third-person omniscient _____
   _____

Skills Practice

Base your answer to questions 6 and 7 on the paragraph below and the lesson content.

Kate thought if the judges did not make up their minds soon, she would pass out from anxiety. Kate did not want to admit that she was afraid to lose the competition; she had worked so hard to get to this place. But little did she realize that Tomas and Jonah were as anxious as she. They just had different ways of showing it. Jonah tapped his feet as if he could make the time go faster. In back of her, Tomas was scribbling along in that notebook he always carried—"Practice, practice, practice" was his motto. All three were the top art students in the school—but after today, only one would be recognized as the best.

6. What is the point of view of this story?
   _____
   _____

7. What words or phrases help you know the story's point of view?
   _____
   _____

Key Terms

character

characterization

direct characterization

indirect characterization

major character

minor character

Characters move a plot forward and help give a story meaning. This lesson will help you learn to analyze characters and interpret their roles in a story.

Characters, Major and Minor

A **character** is a person or role within a story. A **major character** is one who is important to the story. The person you might think of as the hero or villain of a story is a major character. Without the major character, a story cannot develop.

A **minor character**, on the other hand, is less important to the story. The purpose of a minor character might be one or more of the following:

- to give a story atmosphere [*The town was full of cowboys who were up to no good.*]
- to move the plot forward [*The hero bought an apple from the grocer before his journey.*]
- to help describe other characters [*Unlike his brother, John was going places.*]

Read the following paragraph from a short story:

> Miguel squinted into the sun; it was going to be another dry, dusty, and very hot day. He felt the reins in his hand tug; his horse, ever impatient, was ready for the day's work ahead. He heard Mr. Ramirez, his back ramrod straight in the saddle, talking to the other cowboys; you could see from the way they stood around him that he was the boss. Something about the way Mr. Ramirez moved and talked made people obey, no questions asked. Miguel turned and saw the other new boy, Eli, walking his horse over to the wagon, where he and Hector the cook began talking rapidly—something about dinner. The two laughed heartily.

Miguel seems to be the main character. Both Miguel and Mr. Ramirez are described more fully than Eli and Hector, about whom the reader knows little. Eli and Hector seem to have minor roles in this story so far.

Direct and Indirect Characterization

Characterization is the way a character's personality is described in a story. Characterization can be direct. In **direct characterization**, the narrator tells the reader directly how a character looks, acts, or feels.

- *He was short.*
- *She was friendly.*
- *They were suspicious of others.*

Characterization can also be indirect: the author provides details, and the reader must determine what these details mean about a character.

Methods of **indirect characterization** can include the following:

- How a character speaks: Does he have a foreign accent? Does he use large vocabulary words? These offer clues to the sort of person a character is.

- A character's actions: Is a character described as "always taking time to help old people across the street"? A reader might infer that she is kind and patient.

- Descriptions of a character's physical appearance or dress: Is she wearing rags? Does he wear the kind of bright clothes that always draw attention to him?

Read the following paragraph from a short story:

Will sat silently among the trees and rocks in the valley. The only sound he heard was his labored breathing. He kicked at the leather boots and stared at them; when it was safe he would have to find a way to trade down. A pauper wearing nobleman's boots would raise suspicion. With that decided, Will stood and watched as the moon rose over the valley. It was time to move on before the horses caught up with him.

What can you infer about Will? He has "labored breathing." This suggests that he has been running. He is wearing "nobleman's boots." It seems he is a nobleman on the run and has disguised himself as a pauper. All of this information about Will can be determined by the details the author emphasizes and how the author describes them.

Skills Tip

Indirect characterization includes the *tone* with which the author communicates information about a character. A character may be six feet four inches tall, but this may be expressed in one of these tones:

- neutral [*He was tall.*]

- positive [*He was larger than life.*]

- negative [*He was imposing.*]

Complete the activities below to check your understanding of the lesson content. The Unit 1 Answer Key is on page 153.

Vocabulary

Write definitions in your own words for each of the key terms.

1. character _____

_____

2. major character _____

_____

3. minor character _____

_____

4. direct characterization _____

_____

5. indirect characterization _____

_____

Skills Practice

Choose the most appropriate characterization for the character based on the sentence from a short story.

6. Harry spoke like a cheetah that had just spotted its prey.

    A. loud

    B. hungry

    C. aggressive

    D. timid

7. She considered each question like the fate of world peace hung in the balance.

    A. thoughtful

    B. lazy

    C. bookish

    D. poor

8. He wore designer jeans and sunglasses, and he carried himself with an air of "I just got back from Milan."

    A. open-minded

    B. wealthy

    C. argumentative

    D. intelligent

9. When Shanna entered the room, the rest of the class rolled their eyes and prepared for her next lecture.

    A. funny

    B. stylish

    C. bossy

    D. friendly

Plot

The **plot** of a story is the series of related events that gives the story a beginning, middle, and ending. The usual pattern of this series of events is for the author to introduce the characters and setting, establish a problem or conflict, and resolve it by the end of the story. This pattern is called the elements of plot.

Introduction

The introduction of a fictional story establishes the setting and characters. This helps the reader understand who the story is about, and when and where the story is happening. As a result, the reader is better able to follow the plot.

Conflict

Conflict happens when two opposing forces meet. A story can have two types of conflict: external and internal. **External conflict** can be between people in the story, or it can be against larger forces, such as natural dangers. Conflict can also result from an idea or belief in society that the main character is against.

Three types of external conflict are seen:

- Character against character
- Character against nature (weather or animals)
- Character against society (public opinion, behavior, or belief)

Key Terms

climax

conflict

denouement

external conflict

falling action

internal conflict

plot

rising action

Real-World Connection

The plot is what makes a book, story, or movie interesting to read or watch. If a book or movie script is well written, the plot is entertaining and believable even if it's unrealistic, such as in a science fiction movie.

Internal conflict is when the character experiences the conflict, or problem, within himself or herself. Examples include:

- Character against his or her conscience

- Character's wants against his or her needs

- Character's opposing emotions

The Middle

Once the conflict has been established, the **rising action** provides the main body of the story and continues the development of the conflict. The rising action is a series of events that leads to the **climax**, or turning point, of the conflict. At the climax, the problem that was the conflict is resolved. The **falling action** is the continuation of the events that conclude the story.

Denouement

Denouement (pronounced day-new-MAHN) is a French term that means "unknotting." This is the conclusion of the story, often called the resolution because the conflict has been resolved.

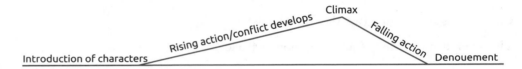

Elements of Plot

Putting It All Together

These elements of plot work together to make a series of people, places, and events a cohesive story. Identifying the elements of plot in a work of fiction as you read makes it easier to follow the story. Notice how the elements of plot are used in the story "Suzanne's Morning Rush."

Suzanne's Morning Rush	
Suzanne knew she was late to work again. Her supervisor would probably glare at her unless she could sneak past the courtesy desk to clock in. Mr. Denning was the newest assistant manager in her store; he had been at a different location before, and the general feeling among the employees was that he was hired to be the serious supervisor. They had nicknamed him "Hatchet."	• *Introduction: The opening establishes the setting and characters.*
Suzanne tried to be on time, but every day something came up. Her dog escaped, or her younger brother refused to get ready for school. He'd miss the bus, and she'd have to drop him off before work. Mr. Denning probably had no life or young children to look after; he just lived for the corporation and looked forward to making his workers miserable by reprimanding them. He was always pointing out her errors until Suzanne thought she couldn't take another moment of his torture. He seldom had anything complimentary to say and always was quick to turn the customers over to her rather than trying to work as a team and offer his help.	• *Rising action/conflict development: The internal and external conflicts become evident.*
When she passed the courtesy desk, Suzanne's eyes were met by Mr. Denning's.	• *Climax: At this point, something in the conflict changes.*
Her anxiety melted as he smiled.	• *Falling action: These events are usually shorter than the rising action.*
"Hello, Suzanne. Is everything going all right for you this morning?" he asked.	• *Denouement: The conflict has been resolved and the story comes to a conclusion.*

Complete the activities below to check your understanding of the lesson content. The Unit 1 Answer Key is on page 153.

Vocabulary

Write definitions in your own words for each of the key terms.

1. plot _____

   _____

2. climax _____

   _____

3. denouement _____

   _____

Skills Practice

Identify whether the following types of conflict are internal or external.

4. character against nature _____

5. character against his conscience _____

6. character against society _____

Place the following five elements of plot in their proper chronological order.

7.

| falling action | rising action | denouement | climax | introduction |

_____

_____

_____

_____

_____

MOOD AND TONE

Identifying the Difference Between Mood and Tone

Mood and tone are very similar because they both deal with feelings. You probably speak of mood and tone every day.

- *Is he in a good mood or bad mood?*

- *He's a moody person.*

- *She spoke to me in a happy tone of voice.*

- *The supervisor's instructions had a sarcastic tone.*

Mood

Mood is the atmosphere or feeling you get when reading fiction. Mood is established through the use of descriptive words about the setting and characters in a story. The writer uses imagery and details that appeal to your senses and draw you into the plot. Feelings such as happiness, anger, joy, and sadness can all be described in detail to give you a feeling of being involved in the story.

> The darkness surrounded her as she sat alone in her room. The silence haunted her until she heard the measured footsteps on the stairs. Her heart seemed to stop beating, and yet her pulse quickened. She held her breath and hoped the alien would not sense her presence.

The phrases "sat alone," "haunted," "stop beating," and "pulse quickened" are descriptions that convey a fearful mood.

Tone

Tone is the attitude of the writer. A writer chooses words and arranges information about characters, events, and ideas to reveal his or her attitude. Examples of the types of attitudes that a writer might try to express are sarcasm, cheerfulness, and pessimism. Tone can be divided into two categories: direct and implied.

- **Direct tone** is when the writer's attitude is clearly stated. A writer sends a letter to the editor of a newspaper revealing her anger about a missing stop sign at an intersection. Your friend expresses a cheerful tone when he signs a text or email with a smiley face. You may use a sarcastic tone when your brother says he'll help wash the dishes later, and you roll your eyes and respond, "Sure, you will!"

- **Implied tone** is not stated directly. Instead, the writer's attitude is suggested or expressed indirectly and must be determined from clues in the text. Look carefully at the words the author uses to describe people, actions, and situations. From those words, you infer the author's tone.

Key Terms

direct tone

implied tone

mood

tone

Real-World Connection

A movie director uses special effects and music to create mood. Think about your favorite horror movie and the music associated with it; imagine what words the director might have used to explain to the composer the effect he hoped to achieve.

An example of implied tone is found in the following passage. Read the passage carefully. How does the writer feel about education in the United States? How can you tell?

> What an outstanding educational system we have in the United States! All students have the opportunity to obtain a higher education, not like third-world countries that put their children to work almost as soon as they can walk. And because students have this opportunity, American parents feel their children are entitled to a college education and must get one, regardless of the children's interests or abilities.
>
> Moreover, educators nationwide have seen fit to encourage all students to enroll in college. After all, every student has been so well prepared in high school that college will be a breeze. Technical courses, such as electronics and plumbing, and the instructors who know how to teach them have been removed from the public education system. Who needs them? It goes without saying that society will be greatly improved when everyone has a four-year degree in liberal arts.
>
> Meanwhile, does anyone know a good plumber?

The writer uses words and phrases like "outstanding," "so well prepared," and "it goes without saying that society will be greatly improved" ironically. That is, the writer means their opposite. So, what can we tell about the writer's tone? The writer is *frustrated* with the current push to make all students attend college regardless of ability or interest; the writer is also *worried* about the shortage of skilled workers, such as plumbers, that may result from this push to a liberal-arts college degree.

Skills Tip

If you have trouble identifying the difference between mood and tone, just remember that mood is the use of descriptive words, usually about the setting, to make the *reader* feel a certain way. Tone is the use of descriptive words that show how the *writer* feels about the subject.

Complete the activities below to check your understanding of the lesson content. The Unit 1 Answer Key is on page 153.

Vocabulary

Fill in the blank with the correct word using either Mood or Tone.

1. _____ is the atmosphere or feeling a reader gets when reading fiction.

2. _____ is the attitude of the writer.

3. _____ can be stated clearly by the writer or expressed indirectly.

4. _____ is more about the setting than the characters.

Skills Practice

Identify the type of mood being expressed in each of the following sentences.

5. The night was moonless and clouded in a haze from the dust blowing into town from the desolate desert.

   _____ (gloomy, anxious, quiet)

6. Ella's mother reached out with her warm, soft hand, wrapping it around hers.

   _____ (trusting, loving, musical)

7. Ramon bounced his leg in an uncontrollable, nonstop motion, the events of the evening revolving in his head.

   _____ (exhausted, excited, amused)

Theme

The **theme** is the main idea of a work of literature. It is the general message the writer is trying to convey about life.

What Theme Is *Not*

To find the theme of a story, it is helpful to rule out what theme is *not:*

- Theme is *not* a plot summary. (A listing of the series of events that make up the rising and falling action of a literary work does not provide any insight into the writer's opinion.)

- Theme is *not* a moral. (A moral, like in a fairy tale, is too simple. The moral of the story is intended to teach a lesson about good and bad behavior rather than expressing a concept.)

- Theme is *not* the subject of the story. (The subject of the literary work is the "who" or "what." It's the main topic that the story is about. An example might be "boy meets girl." Think about "how" and "why" to get to the theme and try to understand the writer's reason for creating the story.)

Determining the Theme

Let's find the theme in "Suzanne's Morning Rush" from Lesson 4, on page 23. Take a few minutes to re-read that story. First, we'll eliminate what the theme is *not*.

- Plot summary: Suzanne is late to work again.

- Moral: People should be on time to work.

- Subject: Mr. Denning is a strict supervisor who is critical of his employees.

Now, how do we determine what the theme *is*?

In a sentence, how can we state the general message the writer is trying to convey about life? That sentence is the theme of the story.

Analyze the story to determine the theme:

- What phrases or ideas are repeated throughout the story? (Suzanne is frequently late and is worried that she is late again.)

- How does the conflict evolve throughout the story? (Suzanne must face Mr. Denning, and he has a reputation of being very strict even before he came to be supervisor at her location. This causes Suzanne's anxiety to build. She thinks of all the times that Mr. Denning has responded to her and her coworkers in a negative way, and she lets her imagination take over.)

- How is the conflict resolved? (When she passes the desk, Mr. Denning does not react in a negative way at all; instead, he asks if everything is all right.)

- What is the theme? (People sometimes worry about things that have not yet happened, causing them to become anxious over nothing.)

Complete the activity below to check your understanding of the lesson content. The Unit 1 Answer Key is on page 153.

Vocabulary

Fill in the blank with the correct word from the word box.

A plot summary	A moral	The subject	The theme

1. _____ is the listing of the series of events that make up the rising and falling action of a literary work.

2. _____ is the central concept that makes a statement about the topic.

3. _____ is intended to teach a lesson about good and bad behavior.

4. _____ is the writer's opinion about that topic.

5. _____ is the writer's larger message about life.

Answer the questions based on the content covered in this unit. The Unit 1 Answer Key is on page 153.

Mr. Butcher's Visit

1   I was twelve years old the summer Mr. Butcher came to take our pictures. It was also the summer I decided to become a photographer.

* * *

2   "He's coming! He's coming! I see the wagon!" my brother Matthew yelled, waving his hands.

3   I remember dashing into the yard, tearing off my apron, my mother's disapproving clucks in my ear. Couldn't she see? This was far more important than shelling peas. All of Custer County was talking about the man who visited the farmers and took their pictures. His name was Solomon Butcher. And today, he was coming to our house—the Bebenak house!

4   I remember vividly the small wagon crawling down the road. It was one of the strangest vehicles I had ever seen: the bed of the wagon was enclosed and topped with a small gable roof. My father told me that Mr. Butcher developed his photographs in the tiny space. I remember seeing painted on the side of the wagon "For T.J. & S.D. Butcher's Picture Album of Custer County."

5   As the wagon slowed, my father and brothers stood by to welcome our guest. A short man with brown hair and a mustache stepped down from the wagon. Next to my tall father and brothers, he looked like a small dancing bear. He had a ready smile with eyes that crinkled when he laughed. He shook hands eagerly with my father, brothers, and uncle. I had tried to find out as much as I could about Mr. Butcher and his photography—but my parents suggested that perhaps I needed to pay more attention to sewing straight seams and sweeping, than to something so scientific and so decidedly unwomanly.

6   Mr. Butcher hurried over to my mother, introducing himself. He admired my parent's soddie—it stood one-and-half-stories tall with real glass windows and wood floors; the top story had been sheathed with lumber board. Mr. Butcher was also quite taken with the family chairs that had been dragged outside earlier in the morning and carefully placed side by side as if waiting for royalty.

7   The chairs.

8   My father had made the chairs when he was a young cabinetmaker's apprentice to his father in Krakow.

His father expected him to carry on the family trade. But my father dreamed of cornfields and prairie grass dancing on the plains. Somehow he convinced my mother that a better world awaited them both. My mother agreed to come to America, but the chairs had to come, too. And somehow, my father made it happen. My mother constantly reminded us of our heritage and good fortunes in America—but the chairs—the chairs were a reminder of her history and her dreams, too.

9   My reverie was stopped as Mr. Butcher clapped his hands and asked for the family to take their places. My parents sat on the chairs—the King and Queen of the Custer County kingdom, I thought as I watched them. Next came some haggling. Matthew wanted his dog in the picture. Mr. Butcher laughed and nodded. Then my brother Alonzo asked if he could have his prize mare stand next to me. Mr. Butcher agreed, all the while setting up a large, bulky box on his tripod. My father, I could tell, was starting to lose his good humor as he asked, "What next? The pigs? The ducks?" My mother hushed him and told him to smile, or at least not look so dark for the camera.

10   We all faced the hot Nebraska sun; Mr. Butcher explained that this would allow enough light for the photograph to be properly exposed. I saw my parents squinting uncomfortably waiting for Mr. Butcher to take the picture. My brothers stood behind me, along with Uncle Paul.

11   We all waited.
And waited.
And waited.
Finally, Mr. Butcher said, "That's it!"

12   Quickly, he whisked the camera away to the wagon to perform his special magic. I walked quickly over to the wagon and did some more waiting of my own. I took in the vista before me: the horizon that seemed to go on endlessly and the prairie grass blowing softly in the wind. It was as if a veritable sea was in motion. Sunflowers and goldenrod looked like they had been painted with the rays of the sun, their bright yellow heads bobbing up and down in the breeze. I then turned my gaze to the fields where my father, uncle, and brothers toiled ceaselessly. Green stalks of corn stood tall and straight—"the farmer's army" Uncle Paul had teased me once. It was a view that I never got tired of.

13   And then I wondered, could this magical landscape be photographed as well?

14   Impatient, now I began tapping my feet, sending dust swirling into the air. I watched as my parents and brothers stood talking. Mr. Butcher was staying for dinner and the night as part of his payment for a photograph of my family.

15   I could see Uncle Paul gesturing towards the fields—work still needed to be done.

16   I ducked behind the wagon even though I heard my mother calling me. Shaking her head, she walked back into the house to finish preparing for the meal.

17   "I think they're gone," I heard behind me. I jumped. And then before my father found me, I blurted out, "Can girls learn how to take a picture?"

18   Mr. Butcher smiled. "I don't see why not. It's true you do not see many women with cameras, but it is not unheard of. My wife has helped me on occasion. But you need to get permission."

19   I knew then that it was a lost cause. I sighed, my face not able to mask my disappointment.

20   Mr. Butcher then said, "Perhaps I can talk with your father."

21   I sighed again.

22   That evening as the potatoes were being passed around the table, Mr. Butcher asked my father if it would be all right for me to take a photograph. My parents looked at each other and then at me. My father started to shake his head, but my mother, gently placing her hand on his arm, murmured quietly, "Remember your dream? Remember mine?" He stopped and looked at me. Then almost imperceptibly, he nodded.

23   The next morning, I was standing on a hilltop surveying the landscape. Mr. Butcher explained how the camera worked. I listened, a dark, dusty cloth covering my head. I could smell sweat and chemicals. It was magical. Peering through the lens of the camera, something shifted inside me. I knew that no matter what it took, I was going to take pictures.

* * *

24   I have taken many photographs since then. But it is still the first photograph I took on that hot, dusty summer day so many years ago that holds the magic for me. I also have the family photograph that Mr. Butcher took. Many of the faces are now alive only in my memories. But

even now, I still remember the thrill of capturing that landscape, that time, that place. And I can carry it with me not just on a piece of glass, but in my heart.

1. When does the story take place?
    A. in the future
    B. several centuries ago
    C. more than a century ago
    D. present day

2. Where does the story take place?
    A. Nebraska
    B. in a royal court
    C. in the desert
    D. Krakow

Write your responses on the lines provided.

3. What is the point of view of the story?

    _____

4. Identify a sentence from the story that offers a clue about its point of view.

    _____

    _____

    _____

    _____

    _____

Identify each character as either major or minor.

5. the narrator (major, minor)

6. the narrator's brother (major, minor)

7. the narrator's father (major, minor)

8. Mr. Butcher (major, minor)

9. Uncle Paul (major, minor)

Write your responses on the lines provided.

10. How is Mr. Butcher characterized?

_____

_____

11. Which specific details about Mr. Butcher help support the reader's impression of him?

_____

_____

12. What mood is established by the author in the introduction?

   A. seriousness

   B. excitement

   C. awe

   D. sadness

13. What type of conflict is evident in this passage?

   A. Character against character

   B. Character against nature

   C. Character against his conscience

   D. Character against opposing emotions

14. When does the climax of the passage occur?

   A. Matthew sees Mr. Butcher arrive.

   B. Mr. Bebenak invites Mr. Butcher for dinner.

   C. Uncle Paul insists on returning to work in the fields.

   D. Mr. Bebenak agrees to allow his daughter to take a photograph.

15. When does the denouement of the passage occur?

   A. Mrs. Bebenak reminds her husband of his dream.

   B. Mr. Butcher admits that there aren't many women with cameras.

   C. The narrator notices the stalks of corn.

   D. The narrator realizes that she would continue to take pictures.

16. Which of the following details helps to reveal the writer's tone?

   A. "Mr. Butcher developed his photos in the tiny space."

   B. "My parents suggested that perhaps I needed to pay more attention to sewing straight seams"

   C. "I could see Uncle Paul gesturing towards the fields"

   D. "I could smell sweat and chemicals"

| introduction | rising action | climax |
| falling action | | denouement |

Match the correct element of plot to the following details.

17. "I remember vividly the small wagon crawling down the road." [4] _____

18. "My father started to shake his head…" [22]

   _____

19. "We all waited." [11] _____

20. "But it is still the first photograph…" [24]

   _____

Write your response on the lines provided.

21. State the theme of the passage in one sentence.

   _____

   _____

   _____

Reading Poetry and Drama

Poetry is a form of creative writing. It is easy to identify a poem when you see the stanzas on the page or hear a rhyme scheme. Although poetry is musical and inspirational, many people shy away from poetry. Determining the meaning of a poem can be challenging.

A drama or a play is another form of creative writing. Like poetry, a play is easy to identify. The playwright not only writes the dialogue for the actors but also writes stage directions. Like a story, a play has plot and character development. Unlike prose, a play is meant to be performed in front of an audience. This unit will help you better understand the elements of poetry and drama.

Watching a live performance allows the audience to empathize with the actors.

Unit 2 Lesson 1   METER AND RHYME IN POETRY

Stanzas

You can often identify a poem by the way it looks on the page. Instead of using paragraphs for division, poets use stanzas. A **stanza** is a division in a poem that consists of two or more (but usually four) lines.

Stanzas usually have the same length, and each stanza follows the same meter and rhyme scheme. Different types of stanzas have unique names. For example, a two-line stanza is called a couplet. A four-line stanza is called a quatrain.

Key Terms

end rhyme

internal rhyme

meter

near rhyme

rhyme

rhyme scheme

rhythm

stanza

Skills Tip

Not all poems use a fixed meter. Some poets prefer to write using the natural rhythm of speech.

Like a paragraph, a stanza focuses on one main idea. In poetry, the main idea may be an emotion, an image, or an action.

Although a stanza brings structure to a poem, it is not unusual for a poem to have a single stanza.

Meter

If you think of poetry as music, you may hear a regular pattern of stressed and unstressed syllables in a poem. In music, meter refers to the system of beats. In poetry, **meter** refers to the pattern of the rhythm of stressed and unstressed syllables.

Read the following sentences aloud. On the right, the stressed syllables are in bold. Clap your hands as you say each stressed syllable.

Last night I saw you dancing.	**Last night** I **saw** you **dan**cing.
Alone at night, I think of you, Bright eyes, a kiss, your warm smile, Remembering how our love grew, And how your memory never fades.	A**lone** at **night,** I **think** of **you,** **Bright eyes,** a **kiss,** your warm **smile,** Re**mem**bering **how** our **love grew,** And **how** your **mem**ory **nev**er **fades.**

Rhythm is often confused with meter. **Rhythm** is the pattern of stressed and unstressed syllables you can hear when reading a poem. When you read the following verse aloud, you will hear the rhythm. Rhythm can also be created with a repetition of the same sound.

> In came a rat
> Chased by the cat
> The rat stole a roll
> And slipped into its hole.

It is easy to hear meter and rhyme in children's verses. Poems should not be read with a sing-song rhythm, but you can use the principles to understand meter.

Rhyme Schemes

Rhyme is the repetition of the same vowel sound. The words *true* and *blue* rhyme, as do the words *baker* and *maker*. Rhymes that appear at the end of each line are called **end rhymes**. Words that rhyme in the middle of a line are called **internal rhymes**. Often times, a poet will use words that do not rhyme exactly. These are called **near rhymes**, or slant rhymes. Read the following stanza and see if you can find the internal rhymes and near rhymes.

> Brave pioneers, crossing mountains and rivers
> Long cold winters, waiting for the sun to reappear
> Huddling near a warm fire, fearing bitter blizzards.

Pioneers, reappear, near, and fearing are internal rhymes, as are *rivers* and *winters*. *Rivers* and *blizzards* are near rhymes.

When you read a poem, you may notice a pattern of rhymes. This is called the **rhyme scheme**. When describing the rhyme scheme of a poem, we mark each line with a letter of the alphabet. All the lines that have the same rhyme receive the same letter.

The blue bird perched on a cherry tree	*a*
Chur-lee, Tura-lee,	*a*
Deep blue against a sea of pink.	*b*
Watching, then swooping, pouncing on its prey.	*c*
The blue bird soared and sang with glee,	*a*
Chur-lee, Tura-lee,	*a*
Feathered visitors on a wooded lake,	*d*
Singing, then hunting, living off the land.	*e*

The rhyme scheme for this poem is *aabc/aade*.

Poets often write about a single experience that moved them.

Complete the activities below to check your understanding of the lesson content. The Unit 2 Answer Key is on page 153.

Vocabulary

Write definitions in your own words for each of the key terms.

1. stanza _____

   _____

2. meter _____

   _____

3. rhyme _____

   _____

Skills Practice

Read the poem, then answer the questions based on the content covered in the lesson.

> Pioneers, moving from one place to another,
> Walking on foot, riding on dusty horses, traveling by wagon,
> Seeking new beginnings, crossing the prairies.
> Looking for adventure.
>
> Pioneer parents, a daughter and brother,
> Loading their wagons, stuffing them with supplies,
> Corn and potatoes, chestnuts and berries.
> Families traveling together.

4. What is the rhyme scheme of this poem?

   A. *abba/abba*

   B. *abcd/aecd*

   C. *abca/deca*

   D. *abab/cdcd*

5. Which of the following words are near rhymes?

   A. another/brother

   B. wagon/supplies

   C. prairies/berries

   D. adventure/together

6. What is the focus of the second stanza?

   A. forms of transportation

   B. animals

   C. family

   D. food

SYMBOLISM IN POETRY

Symbols

Part of understanding a poem is understanding the symbols in the poem. A word used as a symbol has several layers of meaning. A **symbol** can be a person, place, thing, or event that represents more than its literal meaning.

Consider the symbolism of a rose, an object mentioned in many poems. A rose is more than just a beautiful flower. A rose is a symbol of love, honor, or beauty. A red rose might symbolize passion, romance, or eternal love, whereas a white rose might symbolize purity or spirituality.

You are probably more aware of symbols than you know. Consider all the fairy tales you have read. The hero is a white-clad knight who rides in on his white horse. The villain rides a black horse and has a black heart. A red apple or a red hood represents the eventual spilling of blood.

Colors also symbolize emotions. As mentioned earlier, a red rose represents love, but red can also signify anger and hate. Fires are red, so red can also signify war or other dangerous situations.

Analyzing symbols requires you to think about double meanings. Seasons, for example, often represent the stages of life. Spring is youth; summer represents the prime years; autumn is middle age; and winter symbolizes old age. This chart shows a few examples of literary symbols.

Black: power, emptiness, mystery, evil, death	**River or water:** journey, opportunity, purification	**Fox:** trickery	**Harvest:** success, prosperity, abundance
White: purity, peace, innocence, ice, cold	**Sunset:** endings **Sunrise:** new life, beginnings	**Spider web:** entanglement	**Open window or door:** opportunity, possibility
Blue: peace, order, water, cold, contentment, sadness	**Moon:** mystery, eternity, madness **Sun:** life, knowledge	**Dove:** peace, spirituality, messengers	**Closed window or door:** obstruction, narrow-mindedness
Green: hope, nature, envy, greed	**Mountains:** obstacles, grandeur, solidity, strength	**Eagle:** authority, power, freedom	**Smile:** loving, caring, acceptance, trust

Poets use symbols because they can suggest much more with a simple image. Rather than making a direct statement, the poet wants to stimulate emotions in the reader. The reader interprets the poem based on his or her own experiences.

Remember that the meaning of symbols is personal. For example, an owl might symbolize wisdom to one person but death to another. It is essential to look at the context when you analyze a symbol in a poem.

Key Term

symbol

A bouquet of red roses is a statement of love.

Skills Tip

Water can symbolize rebirth or cleansing. As a storm, water foreshadows unfortunate events or defeat. As a soothing shower, raindrops can symbolize growth, helping crops to grow.

Analyzing Symbols

Notice how the references to fire in the following verse evoke feelings of fear and comfort.

> In the forest on a moonless night,
> Fiery eyes dart to and fro,
> I near the fire, pondering my plight,
> Protecting myself from an evil foe.

Although the color red is never explicitly mentioned in this verse, the reader knows that "fiery eyes" are red. Using the context, the reader can assume that the color red represents anger. The foe has fiery eyes, suggesting the foe could be angry or violent. The fiery eyes symbolize destruction or evil. But notice that in the third line, the word *fire* symbolizes something else. The speaker uses fire as a source of security. The warmth of the fire might protect the speaker. The speaker might even use the fire as a weapon.

We know the forest is dark although the poet doesn't directly state it—he implies it by referring to a moonless night. The juxtaposition of the colors red and black suggests an ominous situation.

What association does the poet want you to have with the color green in these lines?

> I tiptoe through the cool morning grass,
> Dewdrops shimmer like sparkling glass.

The reader knows that grass is green. In the second line, the speaker mentions "sparkling glass." We might associate this image with diamonds. The color green and sparkling dewdrops connote, or suggest, wealth or opportunity (money and diamonds). The poet does not directly state that—the reader interprets the meaning. Based on these lines, the poem would most likely be an optimistic poem.

Real-World Connection

Symbols are everywhere! Think of all the symbols in movies. A flash of lightning and a boom of thunder in a horror flick symbolize that the "creature" is up to no good. A broken glass might symbolize the shattering of a relationship. Even names are symbolic: a robot named Eva (similar to Eve) or a villain named Cruella Deville (sounds like "cruel devil") show what the characters represent to the story.

A dove carrying an olive branch is just one of the many visual symbols of peace.

Complete the activities below to check your understanding of the lesson content. The Unit 2 Answer Key is on page 153.

Skills Practice

Match the object on the left with its symbolic meaning on the right.

1. a black bird
2. lion
3. a trip on a river
4. white rose
5. budding trees on a spring day
6. a barren, winter landscape

A. strength and courage
B. omen of bad news
C. youth and rebirth
D. freedom from oppression
E. pure and innocent love
F. nearing the end of life

Read the poem and answer the questions based on the content covered in the lesson.

> All day it did rain
> Filling rivers and creeks.
> Waterdrops trickle off windowpanes
> Like the tears on my face.
>
> Slowly, gray skies turn to pink
> A rainbow reaches across the sky
> Shimmery radiant colors.
> Glorious end to the day.

7. How do the colors reflect the speaker's mood?

_____

_____

8. What symbol does the speaker use to represent promise and optimism?

_____

Key Terms

alliteration

figure of speech

hyperbole

metaphor

onomatopoeia

personification

simile

Sounds and Comparisons

In addition to patterns of rhythm and rhyme, poetry is filled with images. Many of these images delight our sense of sound. Some of the images present comparisons. Comparisons can personalize a poem or encourage the reader to look at something in a different way.

Onomatopoeia

A poet has several ways to appeal to our sense of hearing and make the language musical. One device is called onomatopoeia (on-uh-mat-uh-PEE-uh). It's a difficult word to pronounce, but it is easy to identify. **Onomatopoeia** is a word that imitates or suggests the sound of the word itself. *Buzzing* bees or *quacking* ducks are examples of onomatopoeia. See if you can identify the onomatopoeia in the following lines:

> It was a huge mistake
>> When the slithering snake
>>> Slid up the tree and hissed,
>>>> "What's this?"

Slithering and *hissed* are the onomatopoeic words. Birds that *chirp*, fires that *crackle*, owls that *hoot*, dogs that *howl*, people who *chomp*, leaves that *rustle*, jets that *zoom*—these are all examples of onomatopoeia.

Alliteration

Alliteration is the repetition of the same letter sound in several words. How many words begin with the letter *s* in the following line?

> The slithering snake slid up the tree and hissed.

Three words begin with the letter *s: slithering, snake, slid*. Two of the words begin with *sl*. The repetition of the *s* sound along with the onomatopoeia (*hissed*) create a realistic image of the snake climbing the tree.

Alliteration occurs with the repetition of the same consonant sound. For this reason, you must listen for the sound rather than look at the spelling. Read the following sentence aloud.

> The slithering snake was uncertain of his voice.

This sentence has a more advanced use of alliteration. The *s* sound in the words *uncertain* and *voice* are stressed syllables. Therefore, the words are considered alliterative.

When a consonant sound is repeated in the middle of a word, it is called internal alliteration. The words *sorrow, tomorrow,* and *borrow* all repeat the *r* sound in the middle. Alliterative words do not have to rhyme. *Water, writing,* and *guitar* all have the internal repetitive *t* sound.

Poets use onomatopoeia and alliteration to create different effects. A poet who wants to create a soothing mood might use words with the soft-sounding *s, l,* or *m*. A poet writing about chaos could use the hard-sounding *d, k,* and *t*. Poets use alliteration to draw readers' attention to those words. Alliteration is a tool that is used deliberately.

Skills Tip

Imagery is what gives poetry life. The images appeal to our senses of smell, sound, touch, and taste. Onomatopoeia and alliteration enhance the sense of sound. Read poems aloud to hear how the sounds affect the mood and tone of a poem.

Figures of Speech

If you tell someone you are going to "hit the hay," no one thinks that you are going to put on boxing gloves and start punching hay. "Hit the hay" is a figure of speech that means you are going to go to sleep. A **figure of speech** is based on a comparison. The two most common figures of speech that poets use are similes and metaphors.

Simile

A **simile** is a comparison of two unlike things joined with a connecting word. Similes are easy to recognize if you find the connecting words: *like, as, than, resembles.* In order for a simile to work, the two things that are being compared have to be dissimilar.

If you say, "Ariel's eyes are like mine," you have not made a simile. If you say, "Ariel's eyes are like deep pools of water," then you have made a simile.

Metaphor

A **metaphor** is a comparison *without* the connecting word. "Ariel's eyes are deep pools of water" is a metaphor. We are all very familiar with metaphors: *Your room is a pig pen. You are a gem. Life is a roller coaster. We're toast. You light up my life* . . . and so on.

It might be easy to identify a simile or a metaphor in a poem. The difficult part is figuring out what the poet means by the comparison. Begin by examining the two things being compared. Then think about the comparison; look for common elements and the meaning behind the objects. Let's consider the metaphor "Ariel's eyes are deep pools of water."

We know there is a comparison of *eyes* and *deep pools of water* and that the two objects are different. *Deep pools of water* suggests a dark blue color. The image of a pool suggests that the waters are calm. *Deep* means the waters have depth. We really don't know what lies deep within the waters. So, the metaphor suggests that Ariel has deep blue eyes and that it is difficult to know what Ariel is thinking or feeling.

Skills Tip

When analyzing a poem, look for ways the poet contrasts the images. These contrasts may be unusual. Read the poem several times to help yourself understand the emotion the poet wants you to feel.

Other Comparisons

There are other ways poets use comparisons in poems. When using these literary devices, the poet must be careful. Sometimes personification and hyperbole can create a comic effect the poet did not intend.

Personification can often have a humorous effect.

Personification

Poets like to give inanimate objects and animals human qualities. The literary device that gives human attributes and feelings to things is called **personification**. A tree that whispers and uses its branches as hands, wind that shouts, and flowers that dance are examples of personification.

Phrases such as "love is blind," "opportunity is knocking," or "jealousy reared its ugly head" are also examples of personification.

Why do poets use personification? When poets give life to inanimate objects and ideas, the reader is forced to look at these objects in a new way. For example, it might be easy for a reader to understand the brutality of winter if the poet has given it human qualities. As readers encounter nature or other things in their daily lives, they can look at them more creatively.

In the following children's poem, the poet compares a vacuum cleaner to a wild creature. The poet has personified the vacuum cleaner by giving it human-like qualities. For example, it eats and uses its "eyes" to look. Because the comparison runs throughout the entire poem, it is called an extended metaphor.

> The beast ate everything lying on the floor,
> When it was done, it began looking for more.
> Its long tail curled and its eyes flashed bright,
> It scared the dog and gave him a fright.

Hyperbole

In our daily speech, we often use **hyperbole**, or exaggeration. If you have ever said, "I have a ton of homework" or "I've seen that movie a million times," then you have used hyperbole. Poets often use hyperbole for effect.

If a poet speaks of an "ocean swallowing him," the poet has used hyperbole *and* personification. "Your love shines brighter than the morning sun" is an example of hyperbole *and* a simile. (Notice the connecting word *than*!) Hyperbole is often found in love poems with lines such as "I will love you for all eternity."

Real-World Connection

Browse your local newspaper to find examples of personification. Here are a few headlines:

Wall Street Chokes on Earnings

Wildfires Leap Across Canyon

Thirsty Lakes Get Boost from Rain

Complete the activities below to check your understanding of the lesson content. The Unit 2 Answer Key is on page 153.

Skills Practice

Read the poem. Then answer the items based on the content covered in the lesson.

[1]   A blue bird danced all day with me,

[2]   Chur-lee, Tura-lee,

[3]   Ballerina in a sapphire sky,

[4]   Twirling, diving, then gliding,

[5]   Soaring higher and higher

[6]   into eternity.

1. In which line does the poet use onomatopoeia?

   _____

2. The phrases "danced all day," "sapphire sky," and "higher and higher" are examples of

   _____

3. Which line contains a metaphor?

   _____

4. What two things are being compared by the speaker?

   _____

5. Which line contains personification?

   _____

6. Explain the personification.

   _____

7. The description of the bird "soaring higher and higher/into eternity" is an example of

   _____

Key Terms

adjective

tone

Defining Tone

When you speak, the tone of your voice is part of how you communicate. Your listener might pick up that you are happy if your voice is light and excited. If you are angry, your voice might express your anger by becoming lower and louder than usual. Poems have tone just as voices do. The **tone** communicates the speaker's feelings toward the subject of the poem.

Describing Tone

Tone is described in one word. We usually use **adjectives** that describe feelings or attitudes to describe tone. A poem about a fire could have an angry tone. The tone of a poem about a ghost could be described as scared or frightened. *Sarcastic, friendly, dark, ominous, sad,* and *loving* are a few of the words that might be used to describe the tone of a poem.

Reading the Poem

The first step in identifying the tone of a poem is to figure out what the poem is about. As you read a poem, think about the main subject. Look at these lines from a poem:

> The sky began to magically change before my eyes;
> Brilliant blues scattered to make room for royal reds.

This is a poem about a sunset. A sunset is the subject of the poem, and the tone will describe the poet's feelings about the sunset.

Skills Tip

Many poets write poems to express their feelings about a subject. As you read a poem, think about how the author of the poem feels about what is being described. The word you use to describe that feeling will describe the tone.

Determining the Tone of a Poem

To describe the tone of the poem, you will have to look for clues about how the poet feels about the subject of the poem.

> The sky began to magically change before my eyes;
> Brilliant blues scattered to make room for royal reds.

Consider the words used to describe the subject of this poem. Words like *magically, brilliant,* and *royal* show that the narrator is impressed by the sunset. The tone of this poem could be described as admiring.

Complete the activities below to check your understanding of the lesson content. The Unit 2 Answer Key is on page 153.

Skills Practice

Read the poem and answer the questions that follow.

> In April, cherry blossoms brush the sky in pale pink-white
> Reminding me of all things Home: the warmth, the evening light,
> And how my mother's daffodils would make us laugh and sing
> A host of childhood memories sprout back in early spring:
> Sweet souvenirs returning from those days when all was right.

1. What is this poem mostly about?

   _____

   _____

2. List some words and phrases from the poem that provide clues to the poet's feelings about the subject.

   _____

   _____

3. What word best describes the tone of this poem?

   _____

4. Describe how one of the words or phrases used in the poem helped you determine the tone.

   _____

   _____

THEME IN POETRY

Key Term

theme

Real-World Connection

Song lyrics are similar to poems. Practice identifying themes as you listen to music. What's happening in the song? Is the song about missing a loved one who has gone away? Perhaps you can recognize the themes of love or grief. Try listening for themes in the songs you hear on the radio. You might notice the same themes showing up in songs that sound very different from each other.

Defining Theme

A **theme** is a central idea that is explored in a poem. The theme of a poem should not be confused with the subject of the poem. For example, the theme of a poem about a beautiful oak tree might be "beauty in nature." The subject is the oak tree. The theme is not usually stated directly. A poem can have more than one theme.

Describing Theme

The theme of a poem can usually be described in one word or a short phrase. *Friendship, love,* and *family* are common themes in poetry. Sometimes a theme can be stated as a lesson or idea the poet wants the reader to think about. For example, "crime never pays" and "love is eternal" are themes that can be found in poetry.

Finding the Theme

As you read a poem, first identify the subject. Next, try to answer the question, "What is this poem about?" without naming the subject or things named in the poem.

> The low branches of the tree called to the children,
> Inviting them to climb into a safe space.
> There they could return in their hearts as adults
> And relive their childhood by simply recalling this place.

The subject of this poem is children climbing a tree. Several themes show up in this short poem. Childhood and growing up are two themes explored here. Remember that, while the subject of a poem might be described directly, the theme is something that you have to figure out on your own.

Complete the activities below to check your understanding of the lesson content. The Unit 2 Answer Key is on page 154.

Skills Practice

1. How is the theme of a poem different from the subject?

   _____

   _____

2. How is the theme of a poem usually expressed?

   _____

   _____

Read the poem and answer the questions that follow.

> In April, cherry blossoms brush the sky in pale pink-white
> Reminding me of all things Home: the warmth, the evening light.
> And how my mother's daffodils would make us laugh and sing.
> A host of childhood memories sprout back in early spring:
> Sweet souvenirs returning from those days when all was right.

3. What is the subject of this poem?

   _____

4. How does the narrator feel about the subject?

   _____

   _____

5. What are two themes present in this poem?

   _____

   _____

STAGE DIRECTIONS IN DRAMA

Parts of a Drama

In literature, a **drama** is a written work intended to be performed by actors. A **play** is a drama intended to be performed on a stage. Dramas are made up of **dialogue**, which includes the lines spoken by the actors and stage directions. **Stage directions** are the instructions the author includes to guide the actors in performing the play.

Recognizing Stage Directions

A play looks different from other types of texts. To understand stage directions, you first have to find them. Stage directions are often found in brackets or set apart from dialogue in italics. Stage directions found at the beginning of a play might look like this:

[Wesley and Bryan are seated across from one another at a table in a school cafeteria. Both boys are wearing basketball uniforms. The cafeteria is empty except for the two boys. Wesley is nervous, looking over his shoulder occasionally as he speaks. Bryan appears calm.]

Stage directions can also be found mixed in with dialogue:

WESLEY: *[leaning in closer, in a strained voice]* Is this going to take long? I don't think it's a good idea for us to be seen together right now.

The words in brackets are stage directions that show how Wesley should be speaking.

As you read a drama, picture the action happening on a stage.

Skills Tip

Try to picture in your head what the stage directions are telling you as you read. Imagine an empty stage and fill it in with the details you read. Picturing the scene described will give you a clearer idea of what the author intends for an audience to see. This will help you better understand the play.

Understanding Stage Directions

When reading a drama, the stage directions will give you lots of clues about what is happening in the scene. Stage directions might contain information about the setting of the play. In the first example, the stage directions let you know that this scene is taking place in a school cafeteria. Information about characters can also be found in the stage directions. Before you even read the dialogue, you know that one of the characters, Wesley, has something to be nervous about. In the second example, you see how Wesley's character is supposed to act as he speaks his lines.

Complete the activities below to check your understanding of the lesson content. The Unit 2 Answer Key is on page 154.

Skills Practice

Read the excerpt from a play and answer the questions that follow.

Cast of characters:

Mr. Warren – an architect
Mrs. Warren – his wife
Becky – the Warrens' daughter

Setting: A campground on a summer afternoon. In the foreground are pine trees and shrubs and a pile of chopped logs. On the painted backdrop are blue sky and the shore of a sparkling lake. Mrs. Warren and the child sit, variously, on the ground and on tree stumps with backpacks. Mr. Warren stands center stage.

Mr. Warren: I'll put up the tent, everyone. How hard can it be? I'm an architect. I design buildings far more complicated than this! [He laughs.]

Mrs. Warren: But, darling, we can help.

Mr. Warren: Thank you, no. Camping was my idea. I'll put up the tent. Everyone just relax and enjoy the outdoors.

Becky: But, mom—

Mr. Warren: Becky, please. I'm concentrating. [He empties the poles, spikes, and other parts onto the ground.] Oh, dear.

Becky: But, dad—

Mr. Warren: [holding the instruction booklet] Not now, Becky. Let's see. "Adjoin tent poles, parts A through F, into two support legs by inserting each tapered end into wide end." Piece of cake.

Mrs. Warren: Darling, I think Becky—

Mr. Warren: Hush, please. I'm reading.

Becky: Dad, you're so stubborn! I'm trying to help!

Mr. Warren: "Using elastic ties, secure parts G through M, to crossbar support as shown in Figure B2." Oh, boy. They make it sound easier than it is!

Becky: But, dad!

Mr. Warren: What is it, Becky?

Becky: [pointing stage left] Our campsite is over *there*.

1. Describe the setting of this play based on the information in the stage directions.

   _____

   _____

   _____

   _____

2. Give an example of stage directions in the excerpt that show what one of the characters should be doing while speaking lines.

   _____

   _____

3. How do the stage directions at the beginning help you understand what is happening in the play?

   _____

   _____

   _____

4. What props, or physical items, would be needed to perform this play on a stage?

   _____

   _____

Dialogue in Drama

Key Terms

dialogue

direct characterization

indirect characterization

plot

Most of the text in a play will be made up of dialogue. **Dialogue** is the conversation that takes place between the actors in a play. Dialogue is the words the actors speak. When reading a play, dialogue will usually look something like this:

WESLEY: I didn't mean for this to happen. Surely you can understand!

BRYAN: Just calm down. I'm sure we can come up with a plan to make everything go back to the way it was before you started this mess.

The name of the character speaking the line comes before the text of the line. In a play, the characters are usually speaking to each other, not to the audience.

Reading Dialogue

When you read dialogue, try to picture the character speaking the words. Pay attention to stage directions as you read. Stage directions can tell you more about the ideas and feelings behind the words. Remember that, although you can enjoy reading a play rather than seeing it performed, the play was written to be performed on a stage. Picturing how a performance might look as you read will help you understand the play.

Dialogue and Characterization

Characterization in drama is mostly achieved through dialogue. Read this exchange between two characters in a play:

BRYAN: I always knew I couldn't trust you. Do you remember the time you stole the cookies out of my lunch box?

WESLEY: Do you mean when we were in kindergarten? Yes, I remember that. I also remember the time you tore up my math homework on the bus.

What are some of the things we can tell about these characters based only on these lines of dialogue? First, we can see that the two characters do not trust each other. We also know that they are the same age. Often the author will tell you directly things about the characters in dialogue. This is called **direct characterization**. In these lines, the author tells the audience directly that Bryan does not trust Wesley. In the following lines, it is implied that Wesley does not trust Bryan. This is **indirect characterization**.

What the characters in a drama say to each other is called dialogue.

Plot and Setting Clues in Dialogue

What happens in a story or play is called the **plot**. The plot includes the events that take place and the actions that occur in a play. In a short story, you have a narrator to tell you what is happening. In a play, you have only dialogue and brief stage directions. The plot of a play is revealed through the dialogue. The characters' words tell you what they are doing and how they feel. This is where you find clues about the main conflict and resolution.

Look for clues about the setting that have been hidden in the dialogue. These clues can help you better picture what is happening. For example, if one character mentions to another that it will be dark soon, you will know the action in that point of the play is taking place in the evening.

Real-World Connection

Some movies and television shows are examples of dramas that you might encounter in your daily life. Pay attention to the dialogue as you watch a television show. Think about how the dialogue would look on a written page. Pay attention to what the dialogue tells you about the characters. Notice direct and indirect characterization in dialogue while watching your favorite television show. How does the dialogue reinforce what you already know about your favorite characters?

Complete the activity below to check your understanding of the lesson content. The Unit 2 Answer Key is on page 154.

Skills Practice

Read the excerpt from a play and answer the questions that follow.

Cast of characters:

Mr. Warren – an architect
Mrs. Warren – his wife
Becky – the Warrens' daughter

Setting: A campground on a summer afternoon. In the foreground are pine trees and shrubs and a pile of chopped logs. On the painted backdrop are blue sky and the shore of a sparkling lake. Mrs. Warren and the child sit, variously, on the ground and on tree stumps with backpacks. Mr. Warren stands center stage.

Mr. Warren: I'll put up the tent, everyone. How hard can it be? I'm an architect. I design buildings far more complicated than this! [He laughs.]

Mrs. Warren: But, darling, we can help.

Mr. Warren: Thank you, no. Camping was my idea. I'll put up the tent. Everyone just relax and enjoy the outdoors.

Becky: But, mom—

Mr. Warren: Becky, please. I'm concentrating. [He empties the poles, spikes, and other parts on the ground.] Oh, dear.

Becky: But, dad—

Mr. Warren [holding the instruction booklet]: Not now, Becky. Let's see. "Adjoin tent poles, parts A through F, into two support legs by inserting each tapered end into wide end." Piece of cake.

Mrs. Warren: Darling, I think Becky—

Mr. Warren: Hush, please. I'm reading.

Becky: Dad, you're so stubborn! I'm trying to help!

Mr. Warren: "Using elastic ties, secure parts G through M, to crossbar support as shown in Figure B2." Oh, boy. They make it sound easier than it is!

Becky: But, dad!

Mr. Warren: What is it, Becky?

Becky: [pointing stage left] Our campsite is over *there*.

1. Why does Mr. Warren feel that he is most qualified to put together the tent?

   _____
   _____
   _____

2. Write one line of dialogue that has an example of direct characterization.

   _____
   _____
   _____

3. Why is Becky frustrated with her father?

   _____
   _____
   _____

4. To whom is Mrs. Warren speaking in the following line:

   Mrs. Warren: Darling, I think Becky—

   _____

5. What does the following line tell the reader about what is happening in the plot?

   Mr. Warren: "Using elastic ties, secure parts G through M, to crossbar support as shown in Figure B2." Oh, boy. They make it sound easier than it is!

   _____
   _____
   _____

Answer the questions based on the content covered in this unit. The Unit 2 Answer Key is on page 154.

Read the following poem and answer the questions based on the content covered in the unit.

Lifting

Grief was a heavy load to bear
But still I lugged it everywhere;
Too dear to shed, too harsh to share,
I bore it silently.

I'd take my load outside and sigh;
Lonely, I'd watch our willow cry.
Its branches hung down from the sky
To weep awhile with me.

And after many weeks of this
I realized my great heaviness
Was lifting, somehow: through some hiss
Of wind and branch and tree.

1. In the first stanza, what metaphor does the speaker use?

   A. Grief is a burden.

   B. Grief is a bear.

   C. Grief is silent.

   D. Grief is treasured.

2. Which literary device best describes the line, "Lonely, I'd watch our willow cry."?

   A. metaphor

   B. personification

   C. hyperbole

   D. onomatopoeia

3. What is the rhyme scheme of the first stanza?

   A. ABAB

   B. ABAC

   C. AAAB

   D. ABCD

4. In the poem, the willow tree symbolizes

   A. unconditional love.

   B. a sympathetic friend.

   C. a reminder of the speaker's loss.

   D. anger and fury.

5. "Hiss of wind" is an example of

   A. alliteration.

   B. rhyme.

   C. hyperbole.

   D. onomatopoeia.

6. Which word best describes the tone of this poem?

   A. loving

   B. skeptical

   C. angry

   D. sad

7. Which of the following describes a theme of this poem?

   A. You never get over losing a friend.

   B. Grief does not last forever.

   C. Loneliness is part of life.

   D. Death is inevitable.

Read the following play excerpt and answer the questions based on the content covered in the unit.

Characters:

Lina: High school student
Kent: High school student
Mr. Lee: Cooking class teacher

Setting: The backdrop displays a classroom set up for cooking class. The actors stand center stage at a table cluttered with culinary supplies.

Mr. Lee: So, fruit salad today? *[points to a bowl of fruit on the table]* Sounds like a real challenge.

Kent: Lina wants us to make homemade jam, actually. But . . .

Lina: All Kent ever wants to do is EAT our ingredients. He already ate half our strawberries.

Kent: Taste testing is an essential part of cooking! And it's June: peach and strawberry season. They're perfect—here, try a peach. *[hands a peach to Mr. Lee]* Anyway, I want to make smoothies. Jam sounds boring.

Lina: You say EVERYTHING is boring.

Mr. Lee: *[through a mouthful of peach]* Neither sounds boring to me, but . . .

Lina: Smoothies are only good on the day they're made! Jam lasts for months.

Kent: *[takes another strawberry]* Smoothies we can share with the class. We don't even have anything to spread jam on.

Lina: Mr. Lee, you're always telling us to try new challenges. Jam is a challenge!

Mr. Lee: That it is. But Kent is on to something. When you have fresh fruit this good, why make it into jam? Why even make it into a smoothie? I say we share it and eat it as it is. Sometimes cooking class isn't about cooking at all. With June's best produce, today is one of those days.

8. Where does this play take place?

   A. in a restaurant

   B. in Lina's dining room

   C. in Mr. Lee's kitchen

   D. in a classroom

9. Lina and Kent cannot agree on

   A. which ingredients to use in the fruit salad.

   B. whether they should make jam or smoothies.

   C. whether they should share their food with the class.

   D. how many peaches to use when making jam.

10. Why does Lina want to make jam?

   A. because it can be shared with the class

   B. because they have fresh ingredients

   C. because it is challenging to make

   D. because they do not have time to make smoothies

Reading Nonfiction

In Unit 1, you learned about fiction. Nonfiction is another type of writing that focuses on facts about people, events, and places that exist in real life, not just in the writer's imagination. There are many types of nonfiction texts. In this unit, you will learn about the different types of nonfiction texts, as well as how to read and evaluate them.

Nonfiction texts contain factual information about real people, places, and events.

TYPES OF NONFICTION

Key Terms

autobiography

biography

memoir

nonfiction

nonfiction prose

review

user manual

Vocabulary Tip

Remember that fiction texts contain stories made up in the mind of the writer. Nonfiction texts can also contain stories, but these stories are about people and places that exist in real life and about events that actually happened.

A **nonfiction** text is one that is based on real facts or events involving real people. Any text that is not fiction, drama, or poetry is nonfiction. Nonfiction texts are everywhere. Newspaper articles, office memos, and user manuals are just a few examples. In this lesson, you will learn about the different types of nonfiction texts you might see in your daily life.

Nonfiction Prose

Nonfiction prose is text that contains facts. As you learned in Unit 1, prose is writing that is made up of sentences and paragraphs without a special structure. Magazine articles, newspaper articles, and textbooks are examples of texts made up of nonfiction prose. Personal essays are also nonfiction prose. The purpose of these texts is usually to inform, but they could also be intended to persuade or entertain.

Biographies and Memoirs

A **biography** is the story of a person's life written by someone other than that person. An **autobiography** is the story a person writes about her or his own life. Like an autobiography, a **memoir** is about the author. However, a memoir might contain only memories and stories from a particular time in the author's life. An autobiography typically covers the author's entire life.

Community and Workplace Documents

You have probably seen notices posted in your community about events, homes for rent, or advertisements for businesses. These documents are posted in public to reach a wide audience. The workplace is another place you will find texts you will need to read and understand. Safety manuals, handbooks, and memos are all examples of nonfiction texts you find in a workplace.

Art Reviews

Many newspapers, magazines, and websites contain reviews of works of art. Movies, books, plays, and albums are examples of works of art that might be reviewed. A **review** is an article that tells the author's opinion of a work of art. For example, your local newspaper might have a review of a play that is running at a theater in your town. A review of a play will usually include a brief synopsis, or summary, of what happens in the play. The writer will usually mention the main characters and actors who play them and give a basic outline of what happens in the play, without spoiling the ending. The writer then gives his or her opinion about the acting and the play itself.

User Manuals

User manuals come with everything from toasters to computers. **User manuals** contain information about products, including instructions for assembling and using them. User manuals usually include a table of contents to show the reader where to find information. Many texts, such as biographies, are meant to be read from cover to cover. User manuals are organized so that readers can find information they need without reading the entire manual.

Real-World Connection

As you go through your day, pay attention to the different types of nonfiction texts you come across. Think about how these different texts are used to relay information and ideas. Compare and contrast the characteristics of different nonfiction texts you see.

Complete the activity below to check your understanding of the lesson content. The Unit 3 Answer Key is on page 154.

Vocabulary

Write definitions in your own words for each of the key terms.

1. biography _____

   _____

2. memoir _____

   _____

3. autobiography _____

   _____

4. user manual _____

   _____

5. review _____

   _____

6. nonfiction _____

   _____

MAIN IDEA AND SUPPORTING DETAILS

The purpose of any nonfiction text is to share ideas and information with the reader. The most important idea in a paragraph or passage is the main idea. The main idea is sometimes stated directly in a topic sentence. The other sentences in a paragraph or passage contain supporting details. Supporting details are made up of information that prove the main idea. In this lesson, you will learn to identify the main idea and supporting details.

Identifying the Main Idea

The **main idea** of a passage or paragraph is the most important idea the author wants to share with the reader. Each reading passage will have one main idea. Reading passages are made up of more than one paragraph. Each paragraph will contain a main idea, too. Often, the author will state the main idea in a **topic sentence**. The topic sentence usually comes at the beginning of a paragraph, but it can be found anywhere.

Read the following paragraph from an employee handbook:

> <u>Beginning August 1, all employees must follow new procedures regarding breaks.</u> Each employee will be required to take a lunch break. Supervisors will schedule lunch breaks at the beginning of each shift. Employees working shifts longer than six hours are also permitted one 15-minute break in addition to their lunch break. This break can be taken at any time. The employee must notify a supervisor before taking a 15-minute break.

The topic sentence of this paragraph, which contains the main idea, is underlined. This sentence tells the reader what the paragraph is mostly about. All of the other sentences in the paragraph contain details about the rules for taking breaks at work.

Identifying Supporting Details

Supporting details are found in the body of a paragraph. Supporting details support the main idea. Supporting details can be made up of any facts, ideas, opinions, or information that supports or proves the main idea. The purpose of the paragraph you just read from an employee handbook is to inform employees about new rules for taking breaks at work. Look at the following sentences from the paragraph:

> *Each employee will be required to take a lunch break.*

> *Supervisors will schedule lunch breaks at the beginning of each shift.*

These sentences contain details that support the main idea by providing information about the new rules for taking breaks at work.

Key Terms

main idea

supporting details

topic sentence

Skills Tip

If the main idea of a paragraph is stated in a topic sentence, try restating the topic sentence in your own words. This will give you a better understanding of the main idea.

MAIN IDEA AND SUPPORTING DETAILS

Evaluating Supporting Details

The supporting details in a paragraph should be directly related to the main idea. If the author includes details that do not support the main idea, the reader might become confused. Think again about the paragraph on break procedures and read the following sentences:

1. There are many restaurants nearby that offer discounts to our employees.

2. Each employee must clock out before leaving for lunch.

Both of these sentences are related to the main idea of the paragraph. However, only one sentence contains information that supports the main idea. The first sentence gives information about where an employee could go on a lunch break. This detail, however, does not give the reader information about the new break procedures. The second sentence instructs the reader on a rule that must be followed. The second sentence should be included in the paragraph.

Using Supporting Details to Determine the Main Idea

Sometimes, the author will not state the main idea directly in a topic sentence. When the main idea is not stated directly, the reader must use the supporting details to infer the main idea.

Read the following paragraph from a letter written by a parent to the principal of her child's school:

> The new school uniforms are only available at one store in town. The store is only open on weekdays until 5:00 p.m. Working parents will have a difficult time getting to the store during business hours to purchase the uniforms. The uniforms are too expensive. Many parents already struggle to pay for school supplies and transportation. This added expense could discourage parents from choosing to send their kids to our school.

This paragraph does not contain a clear topic sentence stating the author's main idea. The author's main message, however, is clear. The main idea of this paragraph could be stated as follows:

New school uniforms will present challenges for parents.

Each sentence in the paragraph contains details that support this main idea.

Real-World Connection

Practice identifying the main idea and supporting details in news articles you read. After you read an article, think about the main idea of the entire article. Next, reread the article and identify the main idea of each paragraph. Think about how the main ideas in the paragraphs support the main idea of the entire article.

Complete the activities below to check your understanding of the lesson content. The Unit 3 Answer Key is on page 154.

Skills Practice

Read the passage. Then answer the questions based on the content covered in the lesson.

Archaeologists rely on human remains and historic sites to understand past cultures and peoples. The most important set of human remains that tells the story of early North American life is the skeleton known as Kennewick Man. The skeleton was found in 1996 by two college students in a narrow part of the Columbia River, near the town of Kennewick, Washington. At first, the skeleton was assumed to be that of a Native American or settler from the 1800s. But a study revealed that Kennewick Man was 9,000 years old.

A legal dispute delayed study of the bones for ten years. Kennewick Man was eventually examined in 2005 and 2006, and the bones revealed unexpected evidence about who he was and how he lived. Several hundred scientists studied the bones, including physical anthropologist Douglas Owsley, of the Smithsonian Institution. The team determined that Kennewick Man was a stocky, muscular man about 5 feet 7 inches tall, weighing about 160 pounds. He was right-handed. His age at death was around 40. So-called CT, or computerized tomography, scans of the limb bones and ribs were taken at the University of Washington Medical Center. Scans like these and other tests revealed he likely hunted with a spear, waded in streams, and ate marine animals such as seals and fish.

The real puzzle was his ancestral origins. Was he Native American, Inuit, or something else? Had he traveled to North America, and if so, how? Owsley believed Kennewick Man belonged to an ancient population of seafarers from Polynesia or Southeast Asia who were America's original settlers, and that Kennewick Man did not belong to any living human population. A group of Native American tribes disagreed. They argued that Kennewick Man was a Native American, and that his remains should be given to them for reburial on their land. In June 2015, scientists from Denmark published a study of Kennewick Man's DNA showing that he is closely related to modern Native Americans. The U.S. Army Corps of Engineers, which controls the land where Kennewick Man was found, currently has the remains. The U.S. Army Corps of Engineers is involved in a number of infrastructure projects throughout the world. The tribes and some public officials have called for the bones to be returned to the Native American tribes.

1. What is the main idea of the first paragraph?

   _____

   _____

2. Based on the information in the passage, what were the physical characteristics of Kennewick Man while he was alive?

   _____

   _____

3. Write the main idea of paragraph 2 in your own words.

   _____

   _____

4. Which sentence in paragraph 3 provides the least support for the main idea and could be deleted?

   _____

   _____

TEXT STRUCTURE

Patterns of Organization

Key Terms

cause and effect

chronological order

compare and contrast

description

problem and solution

text features

text structure

Skills Tip

Problem and solution texts are quite similar to cause and effect. The reader might confuse a problem with a cause. To determine which of the two structures describes the text, find the solution to the problem. The solution may be presented in the body of the text or in the conclusion. If the text contains a solution, the structure is problem and solution. If not, it is cause and effect.

Text structure refers to how a text is organized. Most fiction is organized in **chronological order**. The story has a beginning, a middle, and an end. However, nonfiction text can be structured in a variety of ways. The following chart provides an overview of the different structures and words that signal the type of text structure.

Text Structure	Purpose	Signal and Transitional Words and Phrases
Cause and Effect	Explains why something happened or describes the effects of an event	as a result, because, consequently, since, so, therefore, for this reason
Problem and Solution	States a problem, then offers a solution; proposes an opinion	as a result, because, consequently, the problem is, one reason is, a solution is
Description	Describes features and characteristics of a person, object, or place	for instance, for example, to illustrate, such as
Chronological Order	Tells sequence of events in time order or lists steps in a process	first, next, then, after, before, for a time, when, eventually, finally
Compare and Contrast	Describes similarities and/or differences of two or more things	also, another, in addition to, as well as, similarly, although, but, however, on the other hand, instead of, yet

If you can determine the type of text structure an author is using, you can more easily understand the text. Read the following paragraph and see if you can determine the text structure.

> Genetically modified organisms, or GMOs, are organisms whose genes have been altered. GMOs are foods that are made with genetically altered crops, such as GMO soybeans, corn, or tomatoes. The goal of this practice is to change the structure of a plant in order to increase crop production and create a plant that is resistant to pests.

The author of this paragraph is providing a definition of genetically modified foods. The purpose is to describe the features of GMOs. You may have noticed the phrase *such as*. This is a descriptive paragraph. The main idea of this paragraph is to define GMOs.

Now read the following paragraph. What kind of structure does this author use?

> Consumers have many choices when buying their food. One decision involves the makeup of the food. Genetically modified (GM) foods are made with products that have been genetically modified. Rice that has been altered with vitamin A or tomatoes that have a longer shelf life are GM foods. Organic foods, on the other hand, must be free from genetically modified organisms. Tomatoes and lettuce that are grown without pesticides, artificial fertilizers, and GM seeds are considered organic. Both types of food must follow guidelines for labeling.

This paragraph compares and contrasts two types of foods—GM food and organic food. The main idea of this paragraph is the comparison of the two different kinds of foods.

The organization or structure of a text helps an author present his or her main idea. When you identify the structure of a passage, you can also identify the main idea.

Be mindful that authors can use a combination of text structures. For example, in the preceding paragraph, the author compares and contrasts GM foods and organic foods. If the text were to continue, the author might explain the effects of eating GM foods. In this case, the author has combined two patterns of organization: compare and contrast and cause and effect.

Text Features

In addition to textual structure, nonfiction texts also have unique **text features**. Using these features will also help you understand the author's main idea.

The following is a list of some of the most common text features in nonfiction:

headings	charts	maps
subheadings	diagrams	bold print
side boxes	illustrations	bullets

Chronological and Sequence Writing

Sequence writing explains how to do something. Sequential texts use the same transition words as chronological texts. The difference is that the transition words in a sequential text are used to indicate steps rather than a specific time as in a chronological text.

Complete the activities below to check your understanding of the lesson content. The Unit 3 Answer Key is on page 154.

Skills Practice

Read each passage. Then answer the questions based on the content covered in the lesson.

1. The deer population in inner cities is growing. Regulations prohibit hunting in populated areas. Therefore, deer make themselves at home in cities. They graze on trees, shrubs, and flowerbeds. In the city, deer have no natural enemies. As a result, the deer population increases.

   What is the text structure of this passage?

   A. chronological

   B. cause and effect

   C. compare and contrast

   D. problem and solution

2. It is easy to grow celery from a base. First, chop the celery stalks off the base. Place the base cut side up in a shallow dish of warm water, and then set the dish in a sunny area. After a week, plant the celery base in dirt.

   What is the text structure of this passage?

   A. sequence

   B. descriptive

   C. compare and contrast

   D. problem and solution

3. During the summer months, bats return to the abandoned railroad tunnel. The problem is that people are getting too close to the tunnel and scaring the bats. If the city built a viewing deck, people could enjoy the natural habitat without disturbing the bats.

   What is the text structure of this passage?

   A. descriptive

   B. cause and effect

   C. compare and contrast

   D. problem and solution

4. Hurricanes and typhoons are both cyclones. They are tropical storms that rotate around a low pressure. They both produce heavy rains and high winds. The difference between the storms is their location. Hurricanes originate in the Atlantic Ocean, and typhoons originate in the Pacific Ocean.

   What is the text structure of this passage?

   A. chronological

   B. cause and effect

   C. compare and contrast

   D. problem and solution

Using Prior Knowledge

When you read a text, you do not read it in a vacuum. You approach the text with your prior experience and knowledge. You use your **prior knowledge** to interpret the text—to make sense of it.

Let's say you just read a recent newspaper article about sugar in our diets. You know from past experience and what you have learned from other sources that too much sugar can cause obesity, diabetes, and tooth decay. You also know that people should consume sugar in moderation. As you read the article, you rely on your prior knowledge to make sense of the text.

As you read new information about sugar, you will draw conclusions about the text. You will decide if you think the facts support your prior knowledge. You will also decide if you agree or disagree with the author. When you assess the new information, you **draw a conclusion**.

Read the following passage. What can you conclude about the treasure hunters?

> During a recent dive, treasure hunters found gold coins worth millions. The treasure hunters donated three rare coins to the local museum. In addition, they created a scholarship fund for young people in their community.

Based on their donations to support their community, you probably concluded that the treasure hunters were generous. You made a judgment about the treasure hunters. You also probably concluded that they became wealthy.

When you draw conclusions, make sure they are supported by facts and details from the text. For example, as you read about the treasure hunters, you should not conclude that their find was common.

Making Inferences

Making an **inference** is very similar to drawing a conclusion. Consider the following text.

> Yesterday, children and adults were not playing basketball at the local park. Instead, they were all in the pool, cooling off. Dogs were lying under shady trees, panting, and youngsters were happily slurping on snow cones.

When you read this, you can make an inference. Your inference is that it was a hot summer day. Although the author does not directly state that it was a hot summer day, details in the text let you infer this. Your experience guides you. You know that when people are swimming, dogs are panting, and kids are eating snow cones, it is hot outside.

When you make an inference, you can also predict what might happen based on the facts. Suppose you read an article about an outbreak of the flu. You can infer that more people will be getting sick and that more people will be absent from school and work. You could also infer that more people will be getting flu vaccines. These are all logical inferences. How can you make these inferences? You use your prior knowledge.

Key Terms

draw a conclusion

inference

prior knowledge

Vocabulary Tip

Have you ever heard someone say, "Read between the lines"? It is an idiom that suggests making an inference based on hints or clues. Sometimes we have to "read between the lines" to find out what someone really means.

Real-World Connection

Advertisers want you to make inferences when you watch an ad. When you see someone having a fantastic time drinking a beverage or eating a snack, the advertisers want you to infer that if you buy their product, you too will have a good time.

Read the following passage. What can you infer about the moon based on this passage?

When you look at Earth's moon, you will see craters. These craters were caused by meteors and asteroids slamming into the moon. This activity occurred billions of years ago. Although the moon has volcanoes, the volcanoes are not active. Because the moon has no atmosphere, no weather will affect the moon's surface. In fact, the moon's surface has not changed much in billions of years.

Using the facts from the text, you can infer that the moon's surface is unchanging. You might also infer that the moon's surface is quiet, as no wind is blowing and no rain is falling.

Remember, an inference is a logical guess based on your prior knowledge *and* the text at hand.

What inferences can you make by looking at this photo? What clues from the photo helped you make this inference? How did your prior experience help you make this inference?

Complete the activities below to check your understanding of the lesson content. The Unit 3 Answer Key is on page 154.

Skills Practice

Read the passage. Then answer the questions based on the content covered in the lesson.

The best part of backpacking is being outdoors in nature. After spending all week long working in the noisy city, riding the subway, and staring at computer screens, it is refreshing to escape to the wilderness. Hiking in forests, climbing mountains, and enjoying the sights and sounds—these are events that make life precious.

Some people are afraid of being in the wild. They feel insecure when they are not attached to a cell phone, computer, or television. And forget being away from all the comforts of home! But for me, connecting with nature is bliss. Backpacking is an experience that provides true freedom—freedom and solitude.

1. What can you conclude about the speaker?

   A. He is fussy.

   B. He is honest.

   C. He is athletic.

   D. He is quite old.

2. What does the speaker imply by describing nature?

   A. Backpacking is amazing.

   B. Hiking is a rewarding activity for everyone.

   C. Living in the city is more entertaining.

   D. Connecting with nature is dangerous.

3. From this passage, what can you conclude about backpacking?

   A. It poses risks and dangers.

   B. It requires a lot of planning.

   C. It improves one's health and fitness.

   D. It allows people to connect with one another.

4. What does the passage imply about people who backpack?

   A. They are good with computers.

   B. They are rustic country folk.

   C. They are not loners.

   D. They are not afraid.

Key Terms

author's purpose

description

explain

inform

persuade

Author's Purpose

Authors write for several reasons. Fiction authors write stories or poems to entertain readers. Nonfiction authors write articles to explain, inform, or persuade.

The author's purpose is not the same thing as the main idea. The **author's purpose** is the reason the writer chose to write the text.

Writing to Explain

Authors who write texts that give instructions or teach the reader how to do something are writing to **explain**. Recipes, instructions, owner's manuals, and handbooks are examples of explanatory writing.

Explanatory texts usually include transition words, such as *first, next, then, when,* and *finally.* Look for chronological organization in these texts.

Vocabulary Tip

All authors use **description** in their writing. So, whether you are reading a novel, a social studies textbook, or a recipe, you will find description.

Writing to Inform

If a text includes mostly facts, the author's purpose is to **inform**. Informative writing teaches the reader something about a topic. Textbooks, news articles, biographies, and encyclopedias are examples of informative writing.

Informative texts are factual. They typically use the following text structures:

- compare/contrast
- cause/effect
- order of importance

Informative texts often include precise vocabulary—words that are specific to the topic. For example, an informative text about volcanoes would likely include words such as *magma, crust, molten rock,* and *ash*.

Vocabulary Tip

Denotation is the actual meaning of a word. **Connotation** is the implied meaning or the impression the word leaves on a reader.

Writing to Persuade

Authors who express their opinions are writing to **persuade**. They may want to convince you to believe something, buy something, or do something. Letters to the editor, advertisements, and speeches are examples of persuasive writing.

Persuasive texts provide the author's opinion on a topic. You might find that the author has a critical tone in a persuasive text. The author may use words that have negative connotations.

To determine if an author's purpose is to persuade, look for words in the text such as *should, I believe, bad, good,* and *best.* Look for rhetorical questions and repetition. In addition, persuasive texts are often supported with reasons, evidence, or statistics.

Determining the Author's Purpose

To determine the author's purpose as you read, think about all the skills you have learned thus far.

- Begin by determining the main idea. What is the author saying?

- Next, look at how the author organized the text. What kind of structure does the author use?

- Consider the language the author uses. Is the language casual or formal? Opinionated or neutral?

On standardized tests, you may find a question such as, "What was the author's purpose in writing this passage?" However, questions about author's purpose are not always this clear. The following stems also want you to identify author's purpose.

- Why did the author include lines . . .?

- With which statement would the author most likely agree?

- The author most likely wrote this passage to . . .

- Why does the author include (a quote/a statistic/a study)?

Skills Tip

Persuasive texts often have loaded words. Loaded words produce strong emotional responses. Loaded words stir readers' emotions, either negatively or positively.

Example:
Neutral: *economical*
Loaded positive: *a bargain*
Loaded negative: *cheap*

Unit 3 Lesson 5 | LESSON REVIEW

Complete the activities below to check your understanding of the lesson content. The Unit 3 Answer Key is on page 154.

Skills Practice

Read each passage. Then answer the questions based on the content covered in the lesson.

Remember to check your dog's ears regularly for dirt or wax build-up. To clean a dog's ears, use cotton balls or cotton pads. You can buy a cleaning solution at a pet store or at the vet's office, or you can make the solution yourself. To make a homemade solution, mix one part vinegar with one part water. If the dog's ears are red, it could be a sign of infection, and you should contact your veterinarian immediately.

1. What is the purpose of this passage?

   A. to criticize

   B. to analyze

   C. to entertain

   D. to explain

Mosquitoes are more than annoying. A mosquito bite can lead to severe illness. Some mosquitoes carry the West Nile virus. If the virus is contracted, the bite could cause swelling of the brain, which could be deadly. Other viruses can cause fever, headaches, body aches, and rashes.

2. Why did the author write this passage?

    A. to tell a story about how a mosquito infected a person

    B. to teach readers how to identify a deadly mosquito bite

    C. to inform readers about the transmission of diseases by mosquitoes

    D. to persuade readers that they should wear mosquito repellent

There are those who argue that talking and texting on the phone while driving is not dangerous. They claim that not all drivers are distracted as they text on their phones while driving a two-ton vehicle down the highway. Yet studies conclusively show that the risk of a car crash increases if drivers are distracted while dialing numbers or texting. The truth is that safe driving requires concentration and attention.

3. What is the author's purpose for writing this passage?

    A. to encourage readers that they need to improve their driving skills

    B. to persuade readers that using a phone while driving is dangerous

    C. to explain the opposing views people have about cell phones and driving

    D. to express frustration about careless drivers who text while driving

4. With which statement would the author most likely agree?

    A. There should be a ban on cell phone devices while driving.

    B. Hands-free cell phone devices should be installed in all cars.

    C. Drivers should be required to take behind-the-wheel courses yearly.

    D. Responsible drivers can safely use cell phones while driving their cars.

When you tell a friend what happened at a birthday party, you seldom include every detail of the event. Instead you share the "highlights" of the party; you summarize the most important activities in a few words to let your friend know what he or she missed.

Sorting the Content

A **summary** is a brief statement or restatement of main points; it is often the concluding paragraph of an essay.

When you are asked to summarize a chapter, you are expected to identify the main ideas of the material you have read. You can identify the main idea if you learn to distinguish, or sort, the content into two categories:

- A **generalization** is a broad statement or main idea.

- An **example** is a specific detail that explains or supports the generalization.

    Young men and women in the military learn job skills that they can use long after leaving the armed services. Some soldiers specialize in automotive repair while others may learn communication systems.

The first sentence is an example of a generalization, or broad statement. The supporting details are *automotive repair* and *communication systems*; both are examples of the types of job skills that are taught in the military.

Using Your Own Words

A **paraphrase** is when text is reworded to clarify meaning. You paraphrase when you use your own words to rephrase what is being said. It is similar to a translation of a foreign language.

    When participating in a group discussion, a good listener is patient and attentive to what the speaker is saying. He or she is alert and respectful when the speaker is presenting. Texting, doodling, reading, or talking to someone next to you is considered rude behavior. It is important that you are not a distraction to the person speaking.

A paraphrase of this paragraph is:

People should be polite and respectful when taking part in a group discussion.

Key Terms

example

generalization

paraphrase

summary

Vocabulary Tip

Paraphrase can be a noun or a verb. It is a French word from the 1540s that evolved from Latin *paraphrasis* and Greek *paraphrazein* (from *para-* "alongside" + *phrazein* "to show").

- As a noun: A *paraphrase* will help my younger brother to understand the instructions.

- As a verb: I need to *paraphrase* the instructions so my younger brother can understand the assignment.

Complete the activities below to check your understanding of the lesson content. The Unit 3 Answer Key is on page 154.

Vocabulary

Write definitions in your own words for each of the key terms.

1. summary _____

   _____

2. generalization _____

   _____

3. paraphrase _____

   _____

Skills Practice

Answer the questions based on the content covered in the lesson.

Identify whether the type of content in this sentence is a generalization or an example:

4. Educators sometimes teach more than the subject matter of the classroom lessons.

   _____

5. Mr. Williams taught his students more than math; he taught them responsibility.

   _____

Paraphrase this sentence:

6. Proofreading your essay for English class requires a variety of procedures, including using the computer spellcheck, asking a friend to read it, and reviewing it more than one time.

   _____

   _____

When you take a multiple choice vocabulary test, you will do well if you study. This most likely involves memorizing the meanings of the words. However, learning the meanings of lists of unrelated words usually does not help in long-term vocabulary improvement. More often, we build vocabulary by using context clues as well as roots and prefixes to discover word meanings.

Key Terms

prefix

root

suffix

verbal context

Context Clues

When you read, the clue to the meaning of a word may be the other words around it. This is called **verbal context**. The surrounding words in the sentence or the paragraph offer assistance in determining the meaning of unfamiliar words.

- The successful and *affluent* businessman sailed his yacht to the Bahamas.

  Since he is successful and owns a yacht, we can make the logical guess that he is wealthy. *Affluent* means *wealthy*.

- He knew he shouldn't *jeopardize* his job at the home improvement store by working for the competition on the weekends, but he needed the extra money.

  By working for the competition, we can guess that he might be risking his job. *Jeopardize* means *risk*.

Origins of Words

Most English words are borrowed from another language. A large number of words originated from Latin. Others are French, Old English, or Greek. As people traveled throughout Europe, they enriched their vocabularies with new words from other lands:

- Old English: *home, stone,* and *meat*
- Latin: *candle, fever,* and *lettuce*
- French: *baron, attorney,* and *luxury*
- Greek: *athlete, emphasis,* and *rhythm*

UNDERSTANDING VOCABULARY

Analyzing Words

When you analyze something, you break it into parts. Breaking words into parts will make developing your vocabulary seem easier.

- The main part of a word is called the **root**. It's the core of the meaning.
- A **prefix** is the short element that comes before the main part of the word.
- A **suffix** is the part of the word added after the main part.

Pro–duct–ive [having the power of producing or generating activity] is very different from *se–duct–ive* [having the power of temptation].

By studying what different prefixes and roots mean, you can enlarge your vocabulary. Here are a few examples:

Latin Prefix	Meaning	Examples
ab-	from	absent abduct absolve abnormal
bi-	two	bisect bimonthly bicolor
circum-	around	circumstance circumvent circumference

Greek Prefix	Meaning	Examples
anti-	against/ opposing	antibiotic antifreeze antiperspirant antisocial
dia-	through/ across/ apart	diagram diameter diagnose
hyper-	over/above	hypercritical hypertension hyperventilate

Latin Root	Meaning	Examples
-aud-	hear	audible audiovisual auditorium
-port-	carry	portable import
-rupt-	break	rupture corrupt interrupt

Greek Root	Meaning	Examples
-mon-	one/single	monotone monologue
-neo-	new	neolithic neophyte neonatal
-tele-	far/distant	telegram telepathy telescope

Vocabulary Tip

Be careful! Since some of the meanings of the word parts are ancient and obscure, your logical guess may be inaccurate. Always check the meaning in a dictionary!

Complete the activities below to check your understanding of the lesson content. *The Unit 3 Answer Key is on page 154.*

Vocabulary

Write definitions in your own words for each of the key terms.

1. verbal context _____

   _____

2. root _____

   _____

3. prefix _____

   _____

Skills Practice

Answer the questions based on the content covered in the lesson.

4. Which is the correct meaning of *antiseptic*?

   A. against one's will

   B. against infection

   C. extremely dirty

   D. polluted

5. Which is the correct meaning of *circumnavigate*?

   A. remain stationary

   B. step backward

   C. move forward

   D. travel around

6. Which is the correct meaning of *telemarketing*?

   A. selling or advertising by telephone

   B. shopping on the Internet

   C. delivering supplies

   D. interviewing from home

Answer the questions based on the content covered in this unit. The Unit 3 Answer Key begins on page 154.

1. Bradley is writing a book about his life. What type of book is Bradley writing?

   A. biography

   B. autobiography

   C. review

   D. novel

2. A user manual for a television will contain information about

   A. where to buy the television.

   B. the author's opinion of the television.

   C. how to use the television.

   D. the people who made the television.

Read the following paragraph. Then answer questions 3–13 based on the passage and content covered in the unit.

Many people might think the only people at risk for dehydration during the hot summer months are athletes. But dehydration can be a real problem for anyone outside in hot weather. It can happen whether a person is pushing
[5]   a lawnmower, playing softball, or sitting at the beach. Dehydration occurs when the body loses more fluids than it takes in. In hot weather, this condition is especially common as the body perspires more. That is why drinking more fluids is very important. Moderate dehydration is
[10] usually taken care of by an increased intake of liquids such as water or electrolyte drinks. Severe dehydration is more serious: the person can become feverish and confused and will need to see a doctor. You can combat dehydration in several ways. For example, wear light-colored clothing on
[15] sunny days, and if possible, carry out your activities in the shade. If that is impossible, it may be necessary to move indoors. But the best way to prevent dehydration from happening at all is to drink plenty of fluids before, during, and after any activity.

3. Which of the following best states the main idea of this paragraph?

   A. Dehydration is only a risk during the hot summer months.

   B. Drinking lots of fluids is important when trying to prevent dehydration.

   C. Dehydration can be a problem for anyone outside in hot weather.

   D. Wearing light-colored clothing can help prevent dehydration.

4. Based on the information in the passage, moderate dehydration can be taken care of by

   A. seeing a doctor.

   B. working inside.

   C. resting before activity.

   D. drinking fluids.

5. What does *dehydration* (line 2) mean?

   A. illness

   B. loss of water

   C. physical activity

   D. increase in hot weather

6. What does *perspires* (line 8) mean?

   A. rests

   B. exercises

   C. sweats

   D. competes

7. What does *moderate* mean?

   A. not extreme

   B. extensive

   C. superficial

   D. without preparation

8. What does *feverish* mean?

   A. excited

   B. unresponsive

   C. unhappy

   D. ill

9. What does *combat* mean?

   A. fight

   B. reply

   C. continue

   D. surrender

Identify whether the following sentences are generalizations or examples.

10. You can combat dehydration in several ways.

   _____

11. For example, wear light-colored clothing on sunny days, and if possible, carry out your activities in the shade.

   _____

12. But the best way to prevent dehydration from happening at all is to drink plenty of fluids before, during, and after any activity.

   _____

Write your response on the lines provided.

13. Write a summary of the paragraph.

   _____

   _____

   _____

   _____

Read the following paragraph. Then answer questions 14–16 based on the passage and content covered in the unit.

Maria Sklodowska, better known as Marie Curie, was born in 1867, in Warsaw, Poland. She showed a talent for mathematics and science as a child. As an adult, Curie moved to Paris, France, where she enrolled at the Sorbonne, a famous university. There, she studied physics and mathematics. In 1895, she married Pierre Curie, a French physicist. Her groundbreaking work in the new field of atomic physics earned her two Nobel Prizes for physics and chemistry.

14. What is the organizational structure of this paragraph?

   A. description

   B. problem and solution

   C. cause and effect

   D. chronological

15. Which words from the paragraph help you determine the text structure?

   A. "mathematics and science"

   B. "As an adult"

   C. "a famous university"

   D. "two Nobel prizes"

16. Based on the paragraph, what can the reader infer about Marie Curie?

   A. She was a brilliant scientist.

   B. She was a courageous woman.

   C. She was not an outgoing child.

   D. She was not interested in family life.

Read the following paragraph. Then answer questions 17–19 based on the passage and content covered in the unit.

Curie's great discovery was in her experiments with uranium. She discovered the element radium, which comes from uranium. Curie was convinced that radium could be used for therapeutic purposes in hospitals and healing. Her discoveries led to the development of the field of radiology. Because of Curie's discovery, doctors could diagnose and treat disease in new ways.

17. What is the organizational structure of this paragraph?

    A. chronological

    B. problem and solution

    C. cause and effect

    D. compare and contrast

18. What conclusion can you draw from this paragraph?

    A. Uranium was difficult to find.

    B. Radium had beneficial effects.

    C. Doctors were afraid of radium.

    D. Curie misjudged the dangers of radium.

19. What is the purpose of this paragraph?

    A. to describe how effective radium is

    B. to suggest that Curie was a brilliant scientist

    C. to convince readers that radium is harmful

    D. to inform readers about Curie's discoveries

Read the following paragraph. Then answer questions 20–22 based on the passage and content covered in the unit.

In 1911, Curie attended the Solvay Congress in Physics. Only 18 leading scientists from Europe were invited. At the conference, Curie met a young physicist, Albert Einstein. Like Curie, Einstein showed a talent for physics and mathematics at a young age. Similarly, he was awarded the Noble Prize in Physics. The two scientists remained friends for over twenty-five years.

20. Which text structure does the author use in this paragraph?

    A. compare and contrast

    B. problem and solution

    C. cause and effect

    D. chronological

21. Which word or words from the paragraph help you determine the text structure?

    A. "In 1911"

    B. "the two scientists"

    C. "at a young age"

    D. "Similarly"

22. The most likely reason the author included the information about the Solvay Congress was to

    A. explain how Curie met Einstein.

    B. compare Curie's expertise to Einstein's theories.

    C. inform readers that Curie was a highly respected scientist.

    D. suggest that very few scientists in the 1900s had research.

Grammar and Usage

At work, Ashley sees a notice posted on the board in the break room instructing employees about the upcoming company picnic. The notice states that employees attending the picnic may leave work early on Friday. Immediately, Ashley knows that she can leave work early on Friday to attend the picnic. By following the rules of English grammar and usage, the writer clearly communicated the intended message.

Grammar and usage are tools that help writers make themselves understood by readers. **Grammar** refers to the way words fit together to create sentences. **Usage** describes the traditions governing how speakers and writers of a language use it. This unit will help you to understand the rules of standard English sentences.

PARTS OF SPEECH

Key Terms

adjective

adverb

conjunction

grammar

noun

preposition

usage

verb

Skills Tip

To determine whether a noun is common or proper, ask yourself whether it names a specific person, place, or thing. If so, it is a proper noun and should be capitalized.

When you check over your writing, make sure you've capitalized your proper nouns!

Words in English, as in any language, can be divided into different parts of speech. These parts of speech fit together to produce meaning. This lesson will introduce the basic parts of speech and describe how they are used within sentences.

Nouns

Nouns are words that name things. Those things include people, places, things, and ideas. *Jim* and *brother* are nouns. *School* is a noun, as are *justice*, *the United States*, and *century*.

Nouns can be divided into *common* and *proper* nouns. Common nouns describe general ideas, like *school* or *happiness*. Proper nouns refer to specific things, like *Wilson Elementary School* or *Isaac Thompson*, and are capitalized.

Read the following sentence.

> Last *year*, my *sister Janice* began studying at *college* in our *hometown*.

In the above sentence, *year, sister, Janice, college*, and *hometown* are all nouns.

Verbs

Verbs are action or being words. They show what something does or what something is. *Run, loves, become, communicated*, and *think* are all verbs.

Action verbs can show physical action, like *jump, chase*, or *swim*. They can also show mental action, like *believe, dream*, or *forget*. Being verbs, like *seem, appear, be, become, remain*, and *stay*, show how something is or appears to be.

Read the following sentence.

> My friend Sabrina *seemed* tired last night, but she *danced* almost every dance anyway.

In the above sentence, *seemed* and *danced* are verbs.

Adjectives

Adjectives are words that describe nouns. They provide additional information about them.

Read this sentence.

> My friend picked me up in his car.

The words *friend* and *car* are nouns. To make the sentence more specific, you could use adjectives to describe these nouns: *best friend, old friend, big car, new car*, or *fast car. Best, old, big, new*, and *fast* are all adjectives.

These adjectives aren't necessary to make the sentence work, but each adjective adds information that helps the reader get a slightly different impression of the friend and the car.

Adverbs

In general, **adverbs** are words that describe verbs. They tell readers *how*, *when*, or *where* something was done. For instance, read the following sentences:

My daughter reads *well.*

The adverb *well* tells how the daughter reads.

His mother called him *yesterday.*

The adverb *yesterday* tells when his mother called.

She can nap *anywhere.*

The adverb *anywhere* tells where she can nap.

Like adjectives, adverbs are not necessary to make a sentence function, but they add information that makes sentences more specific.

Many adverbs are formed by adding *-ly* to an adjective: for example, *quietly*, *quickly*, and *sadly* are all adverbs. In almost every case, a word ending in *-ly* is an adverb.

In addition to describing verbs, adverbs can describe adjectives and other adverbs. Read the following sentences.

She made a *beautifully* vibrant painting.

The adverb *beautifully* describes the adjective *vibrant*, telling how vibrant.

They traveled *incredibly* quickly.

The adverb *incredibly* describes the adverb *quickly*, telling how quickly.

In short, if a word describes something besides a noun, that word is very likely an adverb.

Conjunctions

A coordinating **conjunction** links two equal words, phrases, or parts of a sentence to show how they relate.

In the phrase *Sam and Dave*, the conjunction *and* links the two nouns *Sam* and *Dave*.

A conjunction can also link whole parts of sentences. Read this sentence:

I went to the store yesterday, *but* I did not see the owner.

The word *but* is the conjunction that links the two separate ideas.

Skills Tip

The seven coordinating conjunctions can be remembered by the word FANBOYS:

F	for
A	and
N	nor
B	but
O	or
Y	yet
S	so

Subordinating conjunctions link ideas that are not of equal importance in the sentence.

> *Despite* agreeing to attend the party, he didn't show up.

In this sentence, *agreeing to attend the party* and *he didn't show up* are not equally important. *Agreeing to attend the party* cannot stand on its own the way *he didn't show up* can. Therefore, the subordinating conjunction *despite* is used to link this phrase to the rest of the sentence.

Other examples of subordinating conjunctions are *because, since, while, so that,* and *when.*

The third type of conjunction is a correlative conjunction. Correlative conjunctions are easy to identify because they come in pairs.

> *Both* Tom *and* Jane went for a hike.

In this case, the correlative conjunction is *both / and.* Other examples of correlative conjunctions include *neither / nor* and *either / or.*

Prepositions

Prepositions explain a relationship of time or space between a noun and another part of the sentence. In other words, prepositions tell *when* or *where* about another part of the sentence. Look at the example below:

> Patricia did her homework *at* the table *after* lunch.

The preposition *at* tells *where* Patricia was doing her homework. The preposition *after* shows *when* she was doing her homework. The prepositions show the relationship between the nouns *table* and *lunch* and the rest of the sentence.

If you change the prepositions, you change the relationship and the meaning of the sentence. Patricia did her homework *at* the table, rather than *under* the table, for instance. Additionally, she did her homework *after*, not *before* or *during*, lunch.

Complete the activities below to check your understanding of the lesson content. The Unit 4 Answer Key is on page 155.

Vocabulary

Write definitions in your own words for each of the key terms.

1. noun _____

   _____

2. verb _____

   _____

3. adjective _____

   _____

4. adverb _____

   _____

5. conjunction _____

   _____

6. preposition _____

   _____

Skills Practice

Circle all of the conjunctions in each sentence.

7. Because he wanted to arrive at work and start the project early, he would either catch the early bus or take his bike.

8. Although she was exhausted, Tania met her sister at the coffee shop, but she couldn't stay late.

9. Daria and her mom would oversleep that morning, yet they would still arrive in time.

Key Terms

complete sentence

fragment

parallel structure

predicate

run-on sentence

subject

In its basic form, a sentence expresses a complete thought. A sentence can be a statement or a question, but no matter what type of sentence it is, it needs to follow a couple of basic rules.

What Makes a Complete Sentence?

To be complete, a sentence must contain a subject and a predicate.

A **subject** is the person, place, idea, or thing the rest of the sentence is about.

A **predicate** contains a main verb and tells what the subject does or is.

Read this basic example.

> *I walked.*

This is a **complete sentence**: it contains a subject (*I*) and a predicate (*walked*). It makes sense.

We can make sentences longer and more complicated, of course.

> *I and my longtime classmate walked slowly to school together yesterday morning.*

It's the same basic idea, but now there are a lot more words. In this case, the subject is now *I and my longtime classmate*. This is what the sentence is about.

The predicate is now *walked slowly to school together yesterday morning*. This still includes the main verb *walked* and tells what the subject did.

Adding words to make your writing more vivid and specific is a good idea. However, a subject and a predicate are all you actually need to make a complete sentence.

Fragments

A sentence **fragment** is an incomplete sentence. A fragment may be missing a subject or a predicate. For example,

> *My dog and I*

What about your dog and you? What did you do? There is no predicate to make this a complete sentence.

> *Ran along the bank of the river*

Who or what ran along the bank of the river? There is no subject to make this a complete sentence.

What about the group of words below? Is it a complete sentence?

My dog and I walking in the park

It looks like it has a subject, *My dog and I*, and it looks like it has a predicate, *walking in the park*. However, this word group is a sentence fragment because the *-ing* form of the verb *walk* cannot stand on its own as the main verb in a predicate. To make this a complete sentence, you need to add a helping verb: *My dog and I were walking in the park.*

One way to determine whether you have a complete sentence or a sentence fragment is to look at the main verb or verbs. Ask yourself two questions:

1. Is it clear what the subject of the sentence is *doing* or *being*?

2. Is the form of the verb one that needs a helping verb, like *was, were, has,* or *have*?

To fix a sentence fragment, you have several options.

Take the following example:

I was running along the bank of the river. Feeling restless.

1. Combine the two sentences if it makes sense to do so:

I was running along the bank of the river because I was feeling restless.

Feeling restless, I was running along the bank of the river.

2. Add a subject or predicate to make the fragment a complete sentence:

I was running along the bank of the river. I was feeling restless.

Parallel Structure

Parallel structure means that items in a list are the same part of speech or are formed the same way.

This is an example of a nonparallel sentence:

I like to shop, cook, and watching television.

In this sentence, you have three items in a list. To give them parallel structure, just make sure all of them have the same form:

I like to shop, cook, and watch television.

I like shopping, cooking, and watching television.

Real-World Connection

You see sentence fragments in many places:

- advertisements

- magazines

- novels

- short stories

- blogs

Used carefully, sentence fragments can be an effective device in your writing tool kit.

Fragments become a problem, however, when they interfere with a reader's understanding. In most work and school situations, it's best to avoid using sentence fragments.

SENTENCE STRUCTURE

Run-on Sentences

A **run-on sentence** contains two or more independent sentences that are not connected properly—they may lack punctuation, have the wrong punctuation, or lack a conjunction. Run-on sentences can be really confusing to readers.

Look closely at this example:

> *I was moving out of our apartment I saw that we needed to vacuum.*

This sentence contains two independent sentences. Where does the first sentence end and the second one begin? It's not clear.

What happens if we add a comma?

> *I was moving out of our apartment, I saw that we needed to vacuum.*

Now we know where the first sentence ends, but the sentence is still not correct.

There are several options for fixing this:

1. Add a coordinating conjunction:

   I was moving out of our apartment, and I saw that we needed to vacuum.

2. Split the sentence into two sentences:

   I was moving out of our apartment. I saw that we needed to vacuum.

3. Combine the sentences with a semicolon:

   I was moving out of our apartment; I saw that we needed to vacuum.

Skills Tip

Remember that you need both a comma and a coordinating conjunction to join two independent sentences. By itself, neither the comma nor the coordinating conjunction is as strong as a semicolon.

Complete the activities below to check your understanding of the lesson content. The Unit 4 Answer Key is on page 155.

Vocabulary

Write definitions in your own words for each of the key terms.

1. subject _____

   _____

2. predicate _____

   _____

3. complete sentence _____

   _____

4. parallel structure _____

   _____

5. fragment _____

   _____

6. run-on sentence _____

   _____

Skills Practice

Identify the underlined portion of each sentence or phrase with one of the terms in the box below. Write the term on the line for each sentence.

parallel structure	predicate	subject	run-on sentence	fragment

_____ 7. Both my brother and sister <u>wanted desperately to visit the water park on that hot summer day</u>.

_____ 8. On our visit to the forest, my classmates and I saw <u>loons, a napping owl, and many squirrels</u>.

_____ 9. <u>Every last one of my classmates</u> insisted that they had never heard of the movie I mentioned.

_____ 10. <u>Walking whenever she gets the chance</u>.

_____ 11. <u>The sun was shining it was not very hot.</u>

TYPES OF SENTENCES

Key Terms

complex sentence

compound sentence

compound-complex sentence

dependent clause

independent clause

run-on sentence

simple sentence

Every sentence requires a subject and a predicate. Once you have those, you can get creative with sentence length and complexity to create different effects and meanings. In this lesson, we will explore different types of sentences.

Independent and Dependent Clauses

Word groups that contain both subjects and verbs are called **clauses**, and they are divided into two main types:

- **Independent clause**: This can express a complete thought and stand on its own as a sentence.

  Kylie ran a marathon

- **Dependent clause**: This does not express a complete thought and cannot stand on its own. A dependent clause must be part of a larger sentence that contains an independent clause.

  Even though her feet hurt

What happened *even though her feet hurt*? This clause *depends* on having something else in the sentence in order to make sense. It will make sense if you add it to an independent clause to form a complete sentence:

  Kylie ran a marathon even though her feet hurt.

Using Conjunctions

Dependent clauses are often introduced by a subordinating conjunction, a word that signals they are dependent. Examples of subordinating conjunctions include *although, because, since, while, when, whenever, where,* and *wherever.*

Other words that can signal dependent clauses are *that, who,* and *which.*

Simple Sentences

A **simple sentence** is the most basic type of sentence. It consists of exactly one independent clause:

  He would like a trip to Mexico.

He is the subject; *would like* is the verb.

  Tom and Carrie are watching the baseball game and are trying to decide what to do next.

Tom and *Carrie* are the subjects; *are watching* and *are trying* are the verbs.

The sentence below is long. It can't be a simple sentence, can it?

I waited along with my brother at the bus stop for what seemed like over an hour.

This is a simple sentence because it contains only one independent clause. *I* is the subject, and *waited* is the verb.

Compound Sentences

A **compound sentence** has *more* than one independent clause and no dependent clause. The clauses of a compound sentence may be joined with a comma and a coordinating conjunction (*for, and, nor, but, or, yet, so*) or by a semicolon.

He hit a home run, but they lost the game anyway.

Sam went to the movies; Lana saw a play.

Complex Sentences

A **complex sentence** consists of an independent clause and one or more dependent clauses. The dependent clauses below are in *italics*.

Since you can't come to the meeting, I will go instead.

We can leave *whenever he gets here.*

Compound-Complex Sentences

A **compound-complex sentence** consists of more than one independent clause *and* at least one dependent clause—it's basically a compound sentence with a dependent clause or two attached. The dependent clauses below are in *italics*.

Because it was raining, I went to the movies, and you stayed home and read a novel.

I voted for Mayor Coleman, but my friend Sarah, *who doesn't like him much,* voted for his opponent.

Skills Tip

A simple sentence can contain more than one subject or verb—just not two independent clauses. These, for instance, are simple sentences:

- *Yasmin packed her lunch and waited for the bus.* [*Yasmin* is the subject of the verbs *packed* and *waited.*]

- *Yasmin and her brother packed their lunches.* [*Yasmin* and *brother* are the subjects of the verb *packed.*]

- *Yasmin and her brother packed their lunches and waited for the bus.* [*Yasmin* and *brother* are the subjects of the verbs *packed* and *waited.*]

How do you know that the sentence below is *not* a simple sentence?

- *Yasmin packed her lunch, and her brother waited for the bus.* [*Yasmin* is the subject of the verb *packed*; *brother* is the subject of the verb *waited.*]

The sentence above consists of *two* independent clauses.

TYPES OF SENTENCES

Skills Tip

Ways to fix a run-on sentence:

1. Split the sentence into multiple sentences.

2. Make it a compound sentence by adding a comma and a coordinating conjunction or by adding a semicolon.

3. Make it a complex sentence: *My sister wanted to join the soccer team, which I thought was a great idea.*

Run-on Sentences

As you learned in Lesson 2, a **run-on sentence** is a sentence consisting of more than one independent clause that is improperly punctuated. Here are some examples that show how you can correct an incorrectly punctuated run-on sentence.

All of these sentences are incorrectly punctuated and thus are run-on sentences.

My sister wanted to join the soccer team I thought it was a great idea.

My sister wanted to join the soccer team and I thought it was a great idea.

My sister wanted to join the soccer team, I thought it was a great idea.

These sentences are correctly punctuated.

My sister wanted to join the soccer team. I thought it was a great idea. [two sentences]

My sister wanted to join the soccer team, and I thought it was a great idea. [comma and coordinating conjunction]

My sister wanted to join the soccer team; I thought it was a great idea. [semicolon]

Complete the activities below to check your understanding of the lesson content. The Unit 4 Answer Key is on page 155.

Vocabulary

Write definitions in your own words for each of the key terms.

1. simple sentence _____
   _____

2. compound sentence _____
   _____

3. complex sentence _____
   _____

4. compound-complex sentence _____
   _____

5. run-on sentence _____
   _____

Skills Practice

6. Combine these sentences into one compound sentence.

   I turned left. I immediately saw my friend walking toward me.

   _____
   _____

7. Combine these sentences into one complex sentence.

   Travis was scared of the dark. He slept all night in the cabin with the lights on.

   _____
   _____

8. Combine these sentences into one compound-complex sentence.

   The explorers split up at the Mississippi River. One turned south. The other turned north.

   _____
   _____

9. Correct this run-on sentence.

   Mr. Vazquez did not enjoy spending time at the mall, he found the crowds overwhelming.

   _____
   _____

A **comma** is a mark of punctuation that indicates a slight pause in a sentence. When you read aloud, you naturally pause briefly at each comma. In this lesson, you will learn some of the many uses of the comma.

Items in a Series

Commas are used between the items in a **series**. A series needs to have at least three items in it, and it can have many more.

He likes to play *basketball*, *baseball*, and *football*.

Red, purple, yellow, or *blue* is my favorite color depending on my mood.

Notice that a comma follows each item in the series except the very last one.

Introductory Phrases

Commas are used to set off an introductory phrase from the rest of the sentence. An introductory phrase provides additional information about the main part of a sentence.

Let's look at some examples:

> *Drenched in sweat*, the runners crossed the finished line.

> *To get to the mall*, you need to turn left at Anderson Lane.

> *Behind the old oak tree in the back yard*, the children found their lost kitten.

Compound Sentences

Commas are used along with **coordinating conjunctions** (*for, and, nor, but, or, yet, so*) to join the independent clauses of a **compound sentence**.

> I wanted to eat vegetables, *but* Jose wanted to eat fruit.

In this case, the comma and the coordinating conjunction *but* join two independent clauses into a compound sentence.

> Jill played Solitaire, *and* Al read a book, *but* Naomi cleaned her room.

This compound sentence has three independent clauses joined by commas and coordinating conjunctions.

Complex Sentences

Commas are used to set off a dependent clause at the beginning of a complex sentence. Remember that a **complex sentence** consists of one independent clause and at least one dependent clause.

> *Because he arrived too late at the station*, he missed the train.

Key Terms

comma

complex sentence

compound sentence

coordinating conjunction

nonrestrictive phrase

series

Skills Tip

What do you do when a series has only two items? Do you need a comma?

No, you don't. Simply use a coordinating conjunction between the two items. For example:

I am short *but* strong.

Zucchini *and* carrots are his favorite vegetables.

A comma follows the subordinate clause *Because he arrived too late at the station* to separate it from the rest of the sentence. (Note: This rule applies only to dependent clauses at the beginning of a sentence. A dependent clause may appear in the middle or at the end of a sentence, and other punctuation rules will apply in those cases.)

Nonrestrictive Phrases

Commas are used to set off a nonrestrictive phrase from the rest of a sentence. **Nonrestrictive phrases**, sometimes called parenthetical phrases, are not necessary to understand the meaning of a sentence. In other words, a nonrestrictive phrase can be taken out of a sentence without affecting the sentence's meaning. Let's look at some examples.

By the way, did you get my email about next week's meeting?

The class field trip, *our first this year*, was very enjoyable.

Last night's student production of that play was brilliant, *in my opinion.*

Notice that the comma may come before or after the nonrestrictive phrase, or the phrase may be set off by commas both before and after it. Try reading each sentence without the nonrestrictive phrase. See how the basic meaning of the sentence is unchanged?

Greetings and Closings

Commas are used after greetings and closings in friendly letters and emails.

Dear Mrs. Garrett,

Thank you for being a great teacher.

Sincerely,

Thomas

A comma follows the greeting *Dear Mrs. Garrett.* Another comma follows the closing *Sincerely.*

Note: The greeting of a business letter or email is followed by a colon.

To Whom It May Concern:

Dear Tax Assessor:

The closing of a business letter or email is followed by a comma.

Vocabulary Tip

Other examples of friendly openings include *Greetings* and *Hello.*

Other examples of closings include *Yours truly, Regards,* and *Take care.*

Complete the activities below to check your understanding of the lesson content. The Unit 4 Answer Key is on page 155.

Vocabulary

Write definitions in your own words for each of the key terms.

1. compound sentence _____
   _____

2. complex sentence _____
   _____

3. series _____
   _____

4. nonrestrictive phrase _____
   _____

Skills Practice

5. Underline the dependent clause in the following sentence.

   After the rain stopped, the sun came out from behind the clouds.

6. Combine the sentences below into a complex sentence beginning with a dependent clause.

   He went to the movies. He took his dog for a walk.

   _____

   _____

7. Underline the nonrestrictive phrase in the following sentence. How do you know it is a nonrestrictive phrase?

   We stayed in Sedona, a small town in Arizona, for one week on vacation.

   _____

   _____

Punctuation serves all sorts of purposes. Some marks signal the end of a sentence, indicating a question or strong emotions. Other marks join words or groups of words. In this lesson, you will learn about end marks, semicolons, colons, hyphens, and dashes and how to use them in a sentence.

End Marks

Use an end mark—a period, a question mark, or an exclamation point—to signal the end of a sentence.

Use a period to end a sentence that makes a statement. A statement is a **declarative sentence**.

> *I think it will rain today.*

Use a question mark to end a sentence that asks a question. A question is an **interrogative sentence**.

> *How are you feeling today?*

Use an exclamation point at the end of a sentence that shows strong feeling.

> *What a great game that was!*

Semicolons

Use a **semicolon** to connect the independent clauses in a compound sentence.

Writers often use a comma and a coordinating conjunction for this purpose. However, a semicolon can also link independent clauses. Compare the sentences below.

> I am going to a friend's house, *and* I will watch the game there.

> I am going to a friend's house; I will watch the game there.

Notice that when the semicolon is used to join independent clauses, no comma or coordinating conjunction (*for, and, nor, but, or, yet, so*) is needed.

Now, take a close look at the following sentence. Can you figure out why the semicolon is correctly used before the coordinating conjunction *but*?

> My friend Armando, who is a great tennis player, is having a good year; but I don't think he will win the tournament.

When the independent clauses of a compound sentence already contain commas, use a semicolon with the coordinating conjunction that joins the clauses. This helps clearly show the "boundary" between the independent clauses.

Key Terms

colon

dash

declarative sentence

hyphen

interrogative sentence

semicolon

Skills Tip

A common mistake many writers make is using too many exclamation points.

Some writers end almost every sentence with one. Other writers use many exclamation points after a single sentence.

Keep in mind that an exclamation point is used only to communicate *strong* emotion.

For most writing in most situations, use periods. Save those exclamation points for something really important.

Skills Tip

Use a colon between the hours and minutes when you write the time.

Examples:
10:30 a.m.
1:15 p.m.

Note: Military time, also called 24-hour time, does not use a colon between the hours and minutes. Because the numbers do not repeat in military time, you don't need to use *a.m.* or *p.m.*, either. In military time, the examples above would be written as follows: 1030, 1315.

Colons

Use a **colon** to introduce a list or an explanation. A colon usually draws attention to the words that follow it.

> I need to get these at the grocery store: *apples, oranges, and grapes.*

In this case, the colon introduces the list of items.

> I'll always remember my friend's advice about getting a dog: *"The best breed is a border collie."*

Here, the colon connects a quotation to the rest of the sentence. The quotation offers an explanation telling what the friend's advice was.

Hyphens

Use a **hyphen** to form one word from two separate words or word parts.

> a *one–way* street

> a *well–known* politician

In the examples above, two words are hyphenated to become adjectives that describe the nouns that follow them. If these same words follow the noun, they are not hyphenated.

> The street goes *one way* only.

> This politician is *well known*.

Some words are always hyphenated. To be sure if you are writing these words correctly, you need to check a current dictionary. Here are some examples:

mid-1990s	anti-American
self-assured	T-shirt
mid-September	pre-Civil War
all-inclusive	ex-husband
mayor-elect	

Dashes

A **dash** is used to set off a list or to show an abrupt break in thought in written dialogue (the lines spoken by characters in a play or movie).

Cinnamon, honeysuckle, and pine—these are some of my favorite scents.

In this sentence, the dash sets off the list of favorite scents. By setting them off this way, the writer emphasizes the items on the list.

Compare the example above with this: *Cinnamon, honeysuckle, and pine are some of my favorite scents.* Do you hear the change in emphasis?

Here's an example of a line of dialogue with an abrupt break in thought:

I adore you, Gwendolyn—get off me, mosquito—more than words can ever say!

Notice that a pair of dashes is needed to separate the words between them from the rest of the sentence.

Complete the activities below to check your understanding of the lesson content. The Unit 4 Answer Key is on page 155.

Vocabulary

Write definitions in your own words for each of the key terms.

1. semicolon _____

   _____

2. colon _____

   _____

3. hyphen _____

   _____

Skills Practice

4. Complete this sentence with appropriate punctuation.

   Our teacher wants us to work on three skills in class ____ reading ____ writing ____ and speaking ____

5. Explain why a semicolon is correctly used in the following sentence.

   I have a big test in the morning; I need to get enough sleep tonight.

   _____

   _____

The subject and the verb of a sentence must agree in number. **Number** refers to whether a word is singular or plural. **Singular** subjects take singular verbs. **Plural** subjects take plural verbs. Likewise, pronouns in sentences must also agree in number with their **antecedents**, the nouns they are replacing.

Singular Nouns	Singular Verbs
horse	gallops
child	cries

Plural Nouns	Plural Verbs
horses	gallop
children	cry

Singular Pronoun	Singular Antecedents
she	Alicia, Dr. Wallace

Plural Pronouns	Plural Antecedents
they	Joan and Richard, students
their	Joan and Richard's, students'

Subject-Verb Agreement

A verb must agree in number with its subject.

> The *man* with the suit and tie *looks* quite sophisticated.

The singular verb of the sentence, *looks*, agrees with the singular subject, *man*. To determine which word is the subject, find the verb and ask yourself, *Who looks sophisticated?* The *man* looks sophisticated. *Man*, not *suit* or *tie*, is the subject of the sentence.

Read the following sentence.

> The *highway* to the mountains *is* under construction.

In this sentence, the singular verb *is* agrees with the singular subject *highway*. What about the plural noun *mountains*? The mountains are not under construction; the highway is. It is a common error to make the verb agree with a noun that is not the subject.

Sentences that have plural subjects take plural verbs. You may notice that most nouns that end in –s are plural. Yet plural verbs do not end in –s.

> The *administrators attend* a meeting.

> Many *firefighters risk* their lives.

The plural verb *attend* agrees with the plural subject *administrators;* the plural verb *risk* agrees with the plural subject *firefighters*.

> The *mayor and voters* in our community *support* the changes in the law.

In this sentence, the plural verb *support* agrees with the compound subject *mayor and voters*. When a compound subject is joined by *and*, the subject takes a plural verb.

Key Terms

agreement

antecedent

number

plural

pronoun

singular

Skills Tip

When a sentence has a prepositional phrase between the subject and the verb, it is a common mistake to confuse the noun in the phrase with the subject. To correctly determine the verb form, try removing the phrase from the sentence.

> The sandwich with the three cheeses (taste, tastes) delicious.

Remove the prepositional phrase *with the three cheeses*.

The subject of the sentence is *sandwich*. The correct verb form is *tastes*.

Pronoun-Antecedent Agreement

A **pronoun** is a word that takes the place of a noun. An antecedent is the word the pronoun is replacing. The pronoun must agree in number and gender with its antecedent. Singular nouns use singular pronouns; plural nouns use plural pronouns.

Singular Pronouns	Plural Pronouns
he, she, it	they
him, her, it	them
his, hers, its	their, theirs
himself, herself, itself	themselves

When Danny arrived at the park, he noticed the river had risen.

Snakes and lizards are reptiles. They are cold-blooded vertebrates.

My sister wants to own her own bakery shop.

Most of the time, it is easy for native speakers of English to use proper pronoun-antecedent agreement. However, the following singular pronouns often present problems in sentence construction.

Singular Indefinite Pronouns			
anybody	each	somebody	nobody
anyone	everyone	someone	no one

Nonstandard English: *Somebody* left *their* umbrella in the lobby.

Because the subject of the sentence—*somebody*—is singular, the pronoun referring to *somebody* must also be singular. *Their* is a plural pronoun. Instead of *their*, you could use the pronoun *his*, or you might use *her*. Rather than exclude one gender, it is often best to write *his or her* or find another way to write the sentence.

Somebody left *his* umbrella in the lobby.

Somebody left *her* umbrella in the lobby.

Somebody left *his or her* umbrella in the lobby.

Somebody left *an* umbrella in the lobby.

Which pronoun is correct?

Each of the boys took (his, their) time on the test.

Begin by removing the prepositional phrase (*of the boys*). The subject of sentence is the word *each*, a singular pronoun. Of the two answer choices, the singular masculine pronoun *his* is the correct answer.

Skills Tip

There are exceptions to the rules. For example, the indefinite pronouns *some, any, none, all,* and *most* can be singular or plural. To determine whether a singular or plural verb should be used with these pronouns, look at the prepositional phrase that follows the pronoun.

Most of the pie has been eaten.

Has, a singular verb, is used because of the singular noun *pie*.

Some of the students have been photographed.

Have, a plural verb, is used because of the plural noun *students*.

Complete the activities below to check your understanding of the lesson content. The Unit 4 Answer Key is on page 155.

Skills Practice

Choose the verb that agrees with the subject or the pronoun that agrees with the antecedent.

1. Although most of the ice cream _____ melted, one pint _____ still frozen.

   A. has / is

   B. have / is

   C. has / are

   D. have / are

2. Homemade spaghetti and crunchy garlic bread _____ me of my grandmother because _____ used to make _____ every weekend.

   A. reminds / she / it

   B. remind / she / them

   C. remind / she / it

   D. reminds / she / them

3. The turtles near the lake _____ basking in the sun, sunning _____ on the rocks.

   A. enjoy / ourselves

   B. enjoys / itself

   C. enjoy / themselves

   D. enjoys / himself

4. Which revision to an underlined portion would correct these sentences?

   When Clarisa and John <u>were</u> asked to introduce speakers at the company reception, I was shocked. Clarisa <u>mumbles</u> <u>her</u> words, and John speaks too loudly. Fortunately, <u>his or her</u> introductions were a success.

   A. Change *were* to *was.*

   B. Change *mumbles* to *mumble.*

   C. Change *her* to *their.*

   D. Change *his or her* to *their.*

The first word of a sentence is always capitalized. However, words within a sentence often need to be capitalized as well. In this lesson, you will learn some essential rules to help you know when to capitalize certain words.

Common and Proper Nouns

Common nouns name a type of person, place, thing, or idea. **Proper nouns** name a specific person, place, thing, or idea. Proper nouns should always be capitalized. Look at the examples below.

Common Nouns	Proper Nouns
person	Joe, Mr. Lee, Ms. Reynolds
place	Spain, Pittsburgh, Main Street
book	*The Velveteen Rabbit*
religion	Christianity, Islam, Buddhism
building	Empire State Building, Museum of Modern Art
day	Saturday, St. Patrick's Day

Titles Preceding Names

Titles (and their abbreviations) that come before names should be capitalized.

Titles of People
Mr.
Ms.
Mrs.
Dr.
Rev. (Reverend)
Sen. (Senator)
Rep. (Representative)

Mr. and Mrs. Castro will be joining us for dinner this evening.

Here, the titles *Mr.* and *Mrs.* are capitalized, as is the proper noun *Castro.*

Key Terms

common noun

proper noun

Skills Tip

Proper nouns help to make writing more specific and vivid. They help the reader "see" what the writer is describing. Compare the two sentences below.

One day, we went to the museum to see the exhibit about a pharaoh.

Last Sunday, Alicia and I went to the Hibbard Natural History Museum to see the exhibit about Pharaoh Ramses II.

The second sentence gives the reader a much clearer picture of what the writer is describing.

Complete the activities below to check your understanding of the lesson content. The Unit 4 Answer Key is on page 155.

Vocabulary

Write definitions in your own words for each of the key terms.

1. proper noun _____

   _____

2. common noun _____

   _____

Skills Practice

Write out each of the following sentences in the space provided and correct any errors in capitalization.

3. the school is located in dallas, texas.

   _____

   _____

4. dr. anderson helped our friend david with his science homework.

   _____

   _____

5. mr. smith is going to washington, d.c., next week to meet with sen. durbin.

   _____

   _____

6. our teacher mrs. rodriguez traveled to germany and france last year.

   _____

   _____

Verb Tense

The **tense** of a verb indicates the time of an action. The three main tenses are present, past, and future tense. There are also three perfect tenses: present perfect, past perfect, and future perfect. The following chart shows the six tenses of the verb *walk*.

Base Form	Present	Present Perfect	Past	Past Perfect	Future	Future Perfect
(to) walk	walk(s)	have/has walked	walked	had walked	will/shall walk	will/ shall have walked

Regular and Irregular Verbs

The verb *walk* is a regular verb. **Regular verbs** form the past tense by adding *-d* or *-ed* to the base form.

Verbs that do not form the past tense in this way are called irregular verbs. **Irregular verbs** do not follow a set of rules, so it is best to check a dictionary when in doubt. The following chart shows some common irregular verbs.

Base Form	Past	Past Participle
break	broke	(have/has) broken
bring	brought	(have/has) brought
run	ran	(have/has) run
see	saw	(have/has) seen
lie	lay	(have/has) lain
put	put	(have/has) put

The verb *to be* is the most irregular verb of all. *To be* can be a main verb (*I am ready*) or a helping verb (*We are going to the movies*).

Base Form	Present	Present Perfect	Past	Past Perfect	Future	Future Perfect
(to) be	am, are, is	have been, has been	was, were	had been	will/shall be	will/shall have been

Most verbs are regular verbs, so a common mistake is to add *-d* or *-ed* to form the past tense of irregular verbs. *Runned, throwed,* and *sitted* are examples of this kind of error.

Key Terms

active voice

irregular verbs

passive voice

regular verbs

tense

Skills Tip

When a regular verb ends in *-e*, the rule is to drop the final *-e* before adding *-ed.*

    hope—hoped

    suppose—supposed

    tiptoe—tiptoed

Some regular verbs require that you double the final consonant before adding *-ed.*

    hop—hopped

    refer—referred

    commit—committed

Consistency of Tense

The tense of a verb shows time. In some cases, it is necessary to change the order of a verb tense to show the order of events.

> During spring training, the athletes *will review* the plays they *learned* during the winter months.

According to this sentence, the reviewing will happen in the future; the learning happened in the past.

In general, shift verb tenses only when necessary. Otherwise, keep your tenses consistent.

> Jamal *takes* his place at home plate and *waited* for the pitch.

In the sentence above, *takes* is present tense, and *waited* is past tense. The verbs should be consistent for the sentence to make sense. Here are two possible corrections:

> Jamal *takes* his place at home plate and *waits* for the pitch. [The verbs are both in present tense.]

> Jamal *took* his place at home plate and *waited* for the pitch. [The verbs are both in past tense.]

Sometimes, writers make the mistake of shifting tenses within or between paragraphs. This error leads to confusing, poorly constructed paragraphs. See if you can find the inconsistent verb forms in the following paragraph.

> *Last weekend, Nora had decided to visit my house. She arrived early in the morning and wanted to go shopping. The local furniture store was having a sale, and Nora wants to buy a new couch. I was excited about the sale, too, as I will be looking for a new dining room table. It was a good thing Nora and I arrive at the store early, as a mob of people were all standing in line!*

As the events in this passage all happened last weekend, the entire passage should be written in past tense:

> *Last weekend, Nora <u>decided</u> to visit my house. She arrived early in the morning and wanted to go shopping. The local furniture store was having a sale, and Nora <u>wanted</u> to buy a new couch. I was excited about the sale, too, as I <u>was</u> looking for a new dining room table. It was a good thing Nora and I <u>arrived</u> at the store early, as a mob of people were all standing in line!*

Skills Tip

Use past tense to tell about events in the past or to tell about historical events.

Use present tense to state facts or when providing an opinion or analysis.

Voice

Skills Tip

Use passive voice when the actor is unknown:

The diamond was stolen yesterday.

Use passive voice when the actor is not the focus:

Three dolphins were rescued after becoming stranded on the beach.

Do not shift from active to passive voice or passive to active voice in the same sentence.

A verb in the **active voice** emphasizes the subject completing the action.

> Our dog Coco *chewed* the garden hose. [The subject is Coco. Coco performs the action of the verb *chewed*.]

A verb in the **passive voice** shifts the emphasis to what is being done and away from *who* performed the action. The passive voice of a verb always includes a form of the verb *be*.

> The garden hose *was chewed* by Coco. [The subject is *hose*. The hose receives the action of the verb *chewed*.]

In some passive voice sentences, the person or thing that completes the action may be entirely absent.

> The garden hose was chewed to shreds. [Who performed the action? We don't know.]

Generally, active voice is preferred because it makes writing stronger and uses fewer words. However, there are occasions when the passive voice is useful. Consider the following statement:

> Large amounts of trash were dumped into the rivers.

In this example, the passive voice is useful to the writer who doesn't know who dumped the trash, only that large amounts were dumped.

Which of the following sentences is more suitable for a wedding announcement in the newspaper?

> The couple was married on the beach.

> Mr. Jones married the couple on the beach.

The passive voice of the first sentence is preferred because it is not necessary to know who married the couple. The active voice of the second sentence focuses too much attention on Mr. Jones, when the couple should be the focus of a wedding announcement.

Complete the activities below to check your understanding of the lesson content. *The Unit 4 Answer Key is on page 155.*

Skills Practice

Write the correct form of the verb in the parentheses on the line provided.

1. I (invite) _____ my best friend to join me on a trip.

2. Yesterday, we (see) _____ several famous paintings at the museum.

3. Later that night, we (drive) _____ to the sea shore.

4. Tomorrow, we (visit) _____ the planetarium.

Choose the correct verb form and fill in the blank.

5. Sandra runs a mile every morning before she _____ breakfast. (eats, ate, has eaten)

6. As I am pulling out of the driveway, my dog _____ chasing my car down the street! (starts, started, had started)

7. Rewrite the following passive voice sentence into the active voice.

    The accident at the lab was investigated by a team of experts.

    _____

    _____

Improving Your Spelling

The best way to learn the spelling of a word is to pronounce the word correctly, think about how it breaks into **syllables** or sounds, and write the word. When you mispronounce a word, it is easy to spell the word incorrectly. For example, if you say prob•ly instead of prob•ab•ly, you will most likely spell the word wrong.

Another good spelling habit is to sound out the word **phonetically**. That means to say each syllable, or word part, aloud. Rather than trying to say the entire word, focus on each syllable. It is easier to focus on a few letters at time. For example, if you want to spell the word *certificate*, divide the word into syllables: cer/ti/fi/cate.

If you find that you misspell certain words over and over, keep a spelling notebook. Correctly spell the words that you miss and look at them frequently. Study how many syllables they have and pronounce the words aloud.

Spelling Rules

These rules will help you spell, but remember that there are always exceptions to the rules.

Use *i* before *e*, except after *c*, or when the word sounds like *a* as in *neighbor*.

Examples:	achieve, believe, brief, field, niece, piece, thief
	receive, deceive, ceiling, weigh, reign
Exceptions:	weird, either, neither, seize

Drop the final *e* before adding a suffix that begins with a vowel (*a, e, i, o, u*).

Examples:	hope + ing = hoping
	ride + ing = riding
	strange + er = stranger
	noble + er = nobler
	admire + ation = admiration
	guide + ance = guidance
Exceptions:	courage + ous = courageous
	notice + able = noticeable

When adding the suffix *-ness* or *-ly*, do not change the spelling of the original word.

Examples:	kind + ness = kindness	sure + ly = surely
	late + ness = lateness	sincere + ly = sincerely

Exceptions: **For words that end in *y*, change the *y* to *i* before adding a suffix.**

empty + ness = emptiness	easy + ly = easily
happy + ness = happiness	day + ly = daily

This rule also applies to other words that end in *y* when adding a suffix that does not begin with *i*.

Examples:	cry + ed = cried	terrify + ing = terrifying
	pretty + est = prettiest	lazy + ness = laziness

Double the final consonant before adding a suffix that begins with a vowel when one of these conditions exist:

- a single vowel precedes the consonant
- the word is accented on the last syllable

Examples:	drop + ing = dropping	droop + ing = drooping
	stop + ing = stopping	stoop + ing = stooping
	occur + ence = occurrence	
	refer + ed = referred	

Skills Tip

Yours truly is used often as a closing for letters.

Truly is truly unique, because you drop the *-e*.

true + ly = truly.

Skills Tip

When adding a prefix to a word, do not change the spelling of the word itself.

dis + appear = disappear

ir + responsible = irresponsible

pre + view = preview

im + patient = impatient

Skills Tip

Here are a few fun ways to remember the spelling of some tricky words.

Dessert, the sweet treat, has two *s's* because you always want seconds.

The person who runs a school is your *pal*—a *principal*.

There is *a rat* in the middle of the word *separate*.

How can you remember that *develop* does not end in an *e?* Develop your mind to **no** end!

Commonly Misused Words

Some of the words in the chart below are easily confused because they are **homonyms**—words that are pronounced the same way but have different meanings and spellings. Learn the meanings and spellings of the words in this chart.

already at an earlier time; previously **all ready** all are prepared	**accept** to receive or take **except** excluding; unless
altogether completely, entirely **all together** everyone in the same place	**affect** to influence **effect** a consequence or a result
des'/ert a dry, sandy region **des/ert'** to abandon or leave **dessert** the final and often sweet course of a meal	**then** next, afterward **than** used to show comparisons
their plural possessive pronoun, "belonging to them" **there** shows place or location **they're** contraction for "they are"	**choose** select (present tense) **chose** selected (past tense)
hear to listen to or perceive sound **here** at this place	**loose** free or relaxed, unattached **lose** to misplace or suffer defeat
its a possessive pronoun, "belonging to it" **it's** contraction for "it is"	**principal** the head of a school **principle** a rule, theory, or law

Complete the activities below to check your understanding of the lesson content. The Unit 4 Answer Key is on page 155.

Skills Practice

Each sentence below has an underlined word. If the word is spelled correctly, write C on the line provided. If the word is misspelled, write it correctly on the line provided.

1. Did you <u>receive</u> the package that I mailed last week? _____

2. When driving through the work zone, please <u>procede</u> with caution. _____

3. I will have to keep my leg <u>imobile</u> while it is healing. _____

4. The children got into an <u>arguement</u> about whose turn it was. _____

Fill in the blank with the correct word.

5. Several people are submitting _____ essays early. (their, there, they're)

6. The movie about schools in Afghanistan had a powerful _____ on the viewers. (affect, effect)

...e questions based on the content covered in this unit. The Unit 4 Answer Key begins on page 155.

Read the following sentence and match each selected word to its part of speech.

Kara went home after work and made a stunningly delicious dinner.

Word:	**Part of Speech:**
1. made	**A.** noun
2. stunningly	**B.** verb
3. after	**C.** preposition
4. dinner	**D.** adverb

5. Choose the conjunction from the following sentence.

   Ida got her coat from the closet and her hat from the cupboard.

   A. her

   B. got

   C. and

   D. from

Read the following sentences and mark each as either complete or incomplete.

6. Olivia headed to softball practice after work and played incredibly well.

   _____

7. Kevin moved slowly through the room because he was trying not to wake the baby.

   _____

8. The soccer team having not lost a game this season.

   _____

Revise the following sentence fragments to make each one a complete sentence.

9. Piled in stacks in the warehouse.

   _____

   _____

10. Hannah along with her sister and older brother.

   _____

   _____

11. Before we left the house.

   _____

   _____

Read the following sentence and identify each clause listed below as either dependent or independent.

   When April's sister Maria decided to come on the trip, even though she was not interested in camping, April made sure Maria had a good time, and Maria agreed afterward that it had been fun.

Clause:

12. When April's sister Maria decided to come on the trip

   _____

13. even though she was not interested in camping

   _____

14. April made sure Maria had a good time

   _____

15. Maria agreed afterward that it had been fun

   _____

Read each sentence below. Identify each with a type of sentence listed in the box.

| simple   compound   complex |

16. Whenever I watch television late at night, I fall asleep on the sofa.

   _____

17. Our main rival withdrew from the tournament, but otherwise the tournament went on as planned.

   _____

18. Renee retrieved her bicycle from the storage shed, put air in the tires, and rode away.

   _____

19. Choose the sentence that is punctuated correctly.

   A. My sister likes to ride her bike, read books, and spend time with her friends.

   B. My sister likes to, ride her bike, read books, and spend time with her friends.

   C. My sister likes to ride her bike read books, and spend time with her friends.

   D. My sister likes to ride her bike, read books and spend time, with her friends.

20. Using a comma and a coordinating conjunction, combine the sentences below into a compound sentence.

   He wanted to go to the movies. He wanted to finish his homework.

   _____

   _____

21. What is the best way to punctuate the underlined part of the following sentence?

   Call me <u>tomorrow we</u> can discuss our homework then.

   A. tomorrow – we

   B. tomorrow; we

   C. tomorrow, we

   D. tomorrow: we

22. What is the best way to write the underlined part of the sentence?

   We went to two places this <u>morning the</u> grocery store and the post office.

   A. morning. The

   B. morning, the

   C. morning; the

   D. morning: the

Choose the verb form that agrees with the subject or the pronoun that agrees with the antecedent.

23. When Steve makes stew, he _____ hot peppers because _____ make the soup spicy, and he knows I _____ the flavor.

   A. adds / they / like

   B. adds / it / liked

   C. add / he / like

   D. add / them / likes

24. Although Marta and Leo _____ shy, they become quite talkative once _____ relax.

   A. seem / he

   B. seems / they

   C. seem / they

   D. seem / she

Rewrite the following sentences so all words are correctly capitalized.

25. Our Class is going on a field trip to washington, D.C., to visit the Lincoln memorial.

   _____

   _____

   _____

26. Juan and michael interviewed mr. Kristoff for their social studies project on saturday.

   _____

   _____

   _____

Write the correct form of the verb on the line provided.

27. Last night, I (decorate) _____ my house for the occasion.

28. I was surprised when the neighbors (bring) _____ over an apple pie.

Choose the correct verb form to fill in the blank.

29. Jeremiah called his boss and _____ why he would be late for work. (explains / explained, will explain)

30. Don't forget that Tanya _____ us to join her for lunch. (invites / has invited / will have invited)

Each sentence has an underlined word. If the word is misspelled, write it correctly on the line provided. If the word is spelled correctly, write C on the line provided.

31. Did you <u>acheive</u> all your goals this week?

   _____

32. It was a <u>careless</u> mistake, one that I hope never to make again. _____

33. I watched the <u>scaryest</u> movie last night on television. _____

Fill in the blank with the correct word.

34. After Roland combed his hair, he was _____ for his class photo. (already / all ready)

35. Will you please _____ my apology? (accept, except)

Writing a Paragraph

Ian's friend Jeff is applying for a new job. Jeff has asked Ian to write a brief recommendation letter for him. Ian knows his friend would be great at this job, but how can he communicate that in a paragraph? Ian decides to keep it simple. He states his opinion and also includes reasons to support why he thinks Jeff should be hired.

The ability to communicate a clear idea about a topic with supporting evidence is an important skill in many situations. This unit will help you to understand how to write a paragraph that has a clear topic sentence, supports a claim with logical reasoning and evidence, and includes transitions to explain the relationships between ideas.

Unit 5 Lesson 1 — TOPIC SENTENCES

Just as any article or essay you write should have a main idea, so should each paragraph. In a well-written paragraph, we call that main idea a topic sentence. This lesson will help you understand how to write a topic sentence.

Key Term

topic sentence

Topic Sentence

A **topic sentence** is a sentence that states the main idea of the paragraph. A topic sentence usually appears at the beginning of the paragraph. In that position, it helps the reader understand what the paragraph will be about. Sometimes the topic sentence is at the end of the paragraph. In that case, the topic sentence summarizes what the paragraph has been about.

Look at the paragraph above one more time. The first sentence is also the topic sentence of the paragraph. The remaining sentences give more information about, or support, the topic sentence. All the sentences in the paragraph are about the same topic.

Now let's look at a paragraph that needs a topic sentence:

> From artists and writers to activists and politicians, many of America's greatest thinkers contributed to the movement for women's rights. Several events mark key turning points for the cultural and political changes brought about by this movement. Among these, the most significant victory of all was the passing of the 19th Amendment, which in May of 1919 granted women voting rights nationwide.

In order to write a topic sentence for this paragraph, you first need to read through it and think about what its main idea might be. Ask yourself: what main idea is the author addressing?

Notice that the details in the paragraph become increasingly specific. The first sentence refers to the *movement for women's rights*. The next sentence mentions there were *key turning points* associated with the women's rights movement. Finally, the last sentence provides a specific example of one of these turning points: the *19th Amendment* to the U.S. Constitution.

The author's main idea is about the history of the women's rights movement. So, a good topic sentence would make a general statement about this:

> The greater part of the 19th and 20th centuries has seen massive advances toward gender equality in American society.

The phrase *gender equality* refers to the idea that men and women have equal political and social rights. So, this topic sentence effectively shows the main idea of the paragraph. All the other sentences in the paragraph support this topic sentence.

Skills Tip

Think of the topic sentence as a claim that expresses the paragraph's main idea.

Complete the activities below to check your understanding of the lesson content. The Unit 5 Answer Key is on page 156.

Vocabulary

Write a definition in your own words for the key term.

1. topic sentence _____

   _____

Skills Practice

Read the following paragraph carefully and answer the questions that follow.

Moving slaves to free states was highly secretive and very organized. Before the Civil War, thousands of people were involved in the effort. Harriet Tubman was one of the brave and passionate leaders. Tubman personally guided 300 slaves to freedom. The operation came to be called the Underground Railroad. It was the first major road to freedom supported by the Abolitionist movement.

2. Summarize the main details of the paragraph in your own words.

   _____

   _____

   _____

   _____

3. Based on the details, write a topic sentence that you think best identifies the main idea that the author is addressing.

   _____

   _____

SUPPORTING DETAILS

A well-written paragraph presents the reader with a complete idea. This idea is presented by the topic sentence and reinforced by supporting details in the remainder of the paragraph. This lesson will help you understand how to write sentences that contain supporting details.

How Do You Support a Topic Sentence?

As you know, the topic sentence of a paragraph tells what the paragraph is about. The **supporting details** of the paragraph supply more information about the topic. They may describe the topic or tell the steps in the topic's process. In addition, the supporting details may offer reasons or evidence for a topic sentence that is an opinion.

Let's take a look at a topic sentence and some supporting details that a writer could use to form a well-written paragraph.

Topic sentence:

> *The Civil War ended in a complicated way.*

This topic sentence is very general. It leaves the reader with all sorts of questions. What evidence about the topic could the author present to support this claim?

Supporting details:

- *General Lee surrendered on April 9, 1865.*

- *Battles continued to be fought afterwards.*

- *It took time for the news of the end of the war to reach all the soldiers.*

These details support the topic sentence *The Civil War ended in a complicated way.* They give context to the topic sentence so that the reader can better understand why the author states that the war's end was "complicated."

Now look at the complete paragraph below. As you read through it, note how the supporting details help the reader to understand the topic of the paragraph.

The Civil War ended in a complicated way. Historians have long debated its actual end. The Civil War truly ended on April 9, 1865 at Appomattox Courthouse in Virginia. On that day, Confederate Army General Robert E. Lee surrendered to Union General Ulysses S. Grant. These generals, ranked highest in each of their armies, signed papers to officially end the war. Lee's authority made the decision final. Still, many troops had not yet surrendered, and the last battle was not until that May. The rest of the Confederacy surrendered as the news reached them. So, despite the scattered nature of the war's closure, its true end was at Appomattox.

Skills Tip

The details in a paragraph should help explain and support the topic sentence in a logical manner. If you come across a sentence in a paragraph that does not support the topic sentence, it doesn't belong in that paragraph. See if the sentence belongs elsewhere in your essay and move it there. If the sentence just doesn't fit, it needs to be deleted. Each sentence should have a good reason for being in your writing.

Complete the activities below to check your understanding of the lesson content. The Unit 5 Answer Key is on page 156.

Vocabulary

Write a definition in your own words for the key term.

1. supporting details _____

_____

Skills Practice

Read the paragraph below and complete the outline that follows. Write the paragraph's supporting details in your own words.

The Constitution was written in 1787, four years after the American Revolution. However, many Americans felt it was incomplete. After fighting a war for a free nation, people wanted to see their liberties secured. James Madison proposed the Bill of Rights to describe freedoms regarding speech, religion, and more. The Bill of Rights was ratified, or agreed to, in 1791. Amendments to secure rights for people of all races and genders were still many generations away. However, the Bill of Rights paved the way for "liberty and justice for all."

2. Supporting detail: _____

_____

3. Supporting detail: _____

_____

4. Supporting detail: _____

_____

5. Supporting detail: _____

_____

Transitions are words or word groups that are used to connect words, sentences, and even paragraphs. This lesson will help you understand how to use transitions to help a reader see the relationships between ideas in your writing.

How Do Transitions Work?

Writers use transitions to point out the connection or relationship between one sentence or one idea and another. In a way, transitions act like street signs, directing the flow of reading traffic. You probably know the meaning of the street signs below.

However, you may be less familiar with the meaning of transitional words and phrases. Look at the table below to see what some common transitions are signaling.

Meaning	Common Transitions
more information	and, additionally, moreover, furthermore, also
comparison	both, similarly, like
contrast	however, on the other hand, rather
reason for	therefore, so, as a result, because (of), consequently
example	for example, for instance

In this text, you can see an example of a "more information" transition:

> My dog doesn't jump on people, and she seldom barks. *Furthermore*, she always comes when I call. Everyone agrees my dog is very well behaved.

In this example, the word *furthermore* is a transition. The previous sentence gave reasons the dog is well behaved. In the next sentence, the writer wanted to add another reason to support why he thinks the dog is well behaved.

Key Term

transitions

Vocabulary Tip

Different transitions show different relationships. That's why it is so important to choose the right transition to express the meaning you intend. Compare the following sentences:

- *Janet dyed her hair;* consequently, *Linda dyed hers.*
  [Linda dyed her hair as a result of, or in response to, Janet dyeing hers.]

- *Janet dyed her hair;* however, *Linda dyed her hair.*
  [This doesn't make any sense. *However* signals a contrast, but both women dyed their hair. *However* is not the correct transition to use in this sentence.]

- *Janet dyed her hair;* however, *Linda just got hers cut.*
  [Now, *however* is used correctly to contrast the actions of the two women.]

The word *furthermore* signals to the reader that the next sentence will continue providing information about the topic of the paragraph. It adds additional support.

Read these sentences:

Successful students develop good study habits. *For example*, some students take notes of main and supporting ideas in their textbooks.

In these sentences, the phrase *for example* is a transitional device. The sentence before it spoke generally about good study habits. The sentence following it gives an example of a good study habit.

Unit 5 Lesson 3   LESSON REVIEW

Complete the activities below to check your understanding of the lesson content. The Unit 5 Answer Key is on page 156.

Vocabulary

Write a definition in your own words for the key term.

1. transition _____

_____

Skills Practice

Complete each of the following sentences with the most appropriate transition word.

2. My friend finished all the math problems. _____, he also read two chapters in his social studies book.

   A. For this reason

   B. Because

   C. In addition

   D. To demonstrate

3. There are many examples of good people who have won the Nobel Peace Prize. _____, Malala Yousafzai won for her efforts in women's education.

   A. For instance

   B. Thereafter

   C. Nevertheless

   D. In addition

4. First, you stir-fry the meat. _____, you add the vegetables.

   A. For example

   B. Then

   C. However

   D. Yet

5. Tomás does not like to play hockey. _____, he loves to play soccer.

   A. For instance

   B. In addition

   C. On the other hand

   D. To conclude

Answer the questions based on the content covered in this unit. The Unit 5 Answer Key is on page 156.

1. Tessa just realized that this paragraph she wrote is jumbled. Help Tessa by identifying the paragraph's topic sentence.

   (A) Government attempts to remedy the crisis did little to help. **(B)** President Franklin D. Roosevelt, elected in 1932, introduced the "New Deal" to turn the economy around. **(C)** Although the New Deal was very effective, the Depression did not end until World War II. **(D)** Unemployment, hunger, and poverty were on the rise. **(E)** The Great Depression began in 1929 and lasted for more than a decade.

   The topic sentence is sentence _____.

2. Read the paragraph below. Based on these supporting details, write a topic sentence for the paragraph.

   The U.S. government took out significant loans in order to fight World War II. With the money, the government hired businesses to build war supplies. The employees included soldiers and workers like doctors, nurses, and engineers. Industry boomed once again. The U.S. economy began to improve.

   _____

   _____

3. Read the paragraph below. Then choose the sentence that best adds a supporting detail to the paragraph.

> President Franklin D. Roosevelt led the nation into World War II after Japan attacked Pearl Harbor. For the first years of his presidency, he had avoided involvement in the war. Instead, he focused on restoring the economy. But in a surprising twist, it was the war—an even greater crisis—that rescued the nation from the Depression.

A. Roosevelt and other leaders had invested years of government programs and aid in improving the economy.

B. The president asked Congress for a declaration of war following the attack on Pearl Harbor.

C. European allies asked for U.S. support against German aggression during World War II.

D. Americans were encouraged by economic growth in the years immediately before Pearl Harbor.

4. Choose the most appropriate transition word or phrase to complete the following sentence.

> Daniel did not study for his science test. _____, he did not earn a good grade.

A. For example

B. Also

C. For that reason

D. However

Writing an Essay

People write for many reasons. Often, they write to inform, to explain, or to persuade. Whenever you read a movie review, an article about a sporting event, an email for work, an editorial, or a recipe, you are reading expository text—text that informs, explains, or persuades.

Good writers follow a writing process in order to present their ideas clearly and in an organized manner. This process varies somewhat for each writer, but the four main stages are prewriting, drafting, revising, and proofreading. Look at this diagram to learn more about the writing process.

The Writing Process

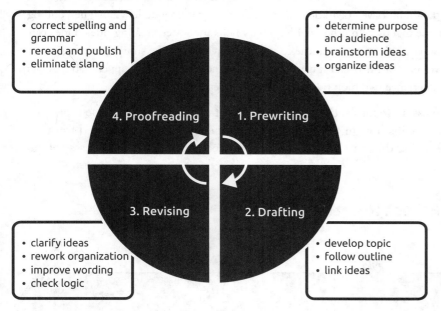

- correct spelling and grammar
- reread and publish
- eliminate slang

- determine purpose and audience
- brainstorm ideas
- organize ideas

4. Proofreading   1. Prewriting

3. Revising   2. Drafting

- clarify ideas
- rework organization
- improve wording
- check logic

- develop topic
- follow outline
- link ideas

Unit 6 Lesson 1 — TYPES OF ESSAYS

Expository Writing

An **essay** is a piece of nonfiction writing that describes, explains, or analyzes a topic. Some essays are informative, whereas other essays provide opinions about the topic.

The purpose of an **expository essay** is to provide information about a topic or to explain something. Expository writing covers a broad range of subjects, from informing readers about history to relating current events, from describing why bees are important to the environment to explaining how to bake a pie or change a tire.

Take a look at the following **informative** paragraph. Notice how the writer **compares and contrasts** facts about Mars and Earth. In this type of organization, the writer discusses the differences and similarities between the two subjects.

Key Terms

cause and effect

compare and contrast

essay

explanatory

expository essay

informative

persuasive essay

Skills Tip

Sometimes it's best to use a graph or a photo instead of words.

Use a visual aid in your essay if:

- you find you are using too many words to explain a simple process.

- your information has a lot of numbers.

- you need a photograph of the real thing.

Remember to label your graphics and position them correctly.

Mars is the planet in our solar system that is most like Earth. Mars, like Earth, has volcanoes, canyons, and polar ice caps. In fact, there are places on Earth that have a similar landscape to Mars. For example, Death Valley, California, with its rocky desert landscape, is similar to what you might see on Mars. Mono Lake, a 700,000-year-old water resource in California, is similar to Gusey Crater on Mars. Volcanoes on the Hawaiian Islands resemble those on Mars, only smaller. Like Earth, Mars also has seasons. Scientists have determined that the seasons on the planet are twice as long as the ones on Earth. This is because an average year on Mars is 687 days, compared to Earth's 365 days. In addition, scientists can determine when a season on Mars is changing by the shifting of its polar ice caps.

There are several ways to present facts and ideas in an expository essay. In the following **explanatory** paragraph about ocean tides, the writer uses description.

The rhythmic rising and falling of an ocean's waters along coastlines are known as ocean tides. To create tides, the ocean depends on help from the sun, the moon, and gravity. Both the sun and the moon have gravitational forces. These forces operate like a magnet, pulling two objects close together. In other words, gravity pulls the water, creating tides. Tides can be high or low. High tides are when the top part of waves reach the shoreline; low tides are when the lower part of the ocean waves hit the shoreline. Ocean tides happen daily; in fact, most coasts experience two high tides and two low tides every day.

Some informative essays focus on the **causes and effects** of a subject. In these types of essays, the writer explains how or why some event happened and what resulted from the event. The following diagram shows how to approach a cause-and-effect essay about volcanic eruptions.

Cause-and-Effect Relationships

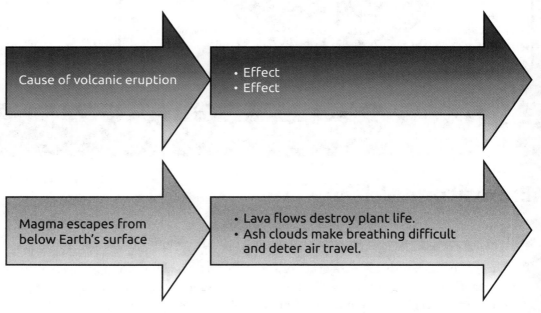

Cause of volcanic eruption

- Effect
- Effect

Magma escapes from below Earth's surface

- Lava flows destroy plant life.
- Ash clouds make breathing difficult and deter air travel.

Persuasive Writing

The purpose of a **persuasive essay** is to provide an opinion about a topic or to encourage the reader to take action. Writers use facts, statistics, and logical reasons to support their opinions. The topic might be serious, such as trying to persuade the readers to vote for a candidate for a government office. Sometimes the topic is less important, such as a movie review.

Read the following letter to the editor and consider the following questions: Who is the audience? What is the topic? What is the writer's point of view? Is the writer convincing?

> To the Editor,
>
> I recently read that the city is planning to cut back on the number of bike lanes on the city streets. I am a student who rides a bike. Like many others, I use my bicycle for different things: I ride my bike to school, I ride to run errands, and I ride because it is fun. Bike lanes are often the only "roads" that keep bike riders safe. Bike lanes clearly mark where the bike riders are supposed to ride. They also help drivers be clear about their lanes too. Taking away the bike lanes will increase the risk of accidents.

The writer is addressing the citizens, in particular, government officials who are in charge of roads. The writer does not support the idea of cutting back on the city's bike lanes. The writer provides several reasons the issue is important to her, but she also emphasizes safety. For this reason, you may view her letter as effective.

Real-World Connection

Advertising relies on persuading people to buy particular products. Advertisers rely on two types of appeals to convince people their products are the best:

- **Logical Appeals:** Use reasons; evidence, such as facts, statistics, expert opinions

- **Emotional Appeals:** Use feelings, descriptive and powerful words, personal examples

However, writing is different from advertising. In order to persuade readers effectively, use strong reasoning and evidence in your writing to support your position.

Complete the activities below to check your understanding of the lesson content. The Unit 6 Answer Key is on page 156.

Skills Practice

Fill in the blank with the correct term from this lesson.

1. An essay that informs the reader is called a(n) _____.

2. An essay that requires the writer to state his or her opinion is called a(n) _____.

Identify whether the purpose of each of the following writing samples is expository or persuasive.

3. Describe why a trip to Florence, Italy, would help your career in art. _____

4. Write a report for your coworkers describing how to use the new computer system. _____

5. Write a letter to your employer about the importance of recycling and the need for recycling bins. _____

6. Write an article for a newspaper describing the lunar landing. _____

PREWRITING

Key Terms

body

brainstorming

conclusion

introduction

prewriting

Brainstorming

Writing an essay can be overwhelming. If you break the task into smaller steps and view writing as a process, you can keep your cool and still write an effective essay.

The first step in writing is **prewriting**. In the prewriting stage, you begin by freely thinking about or **brainstorming** ideas. Determine your purpose. Ask yourself, *What do I want to write about?* Make a list of topics that interest you.

Use free association to write down anything that you know about the topic. That means to write down the first thoughts that come to mind. Ask *Who? What? Where? When? Why?* If you are assigned a specific type of essay, think of topics that are suitable for that type of essay.

For example, if you are asked to write a compare-and-contrast essay, think of two subjects that can be compared easily. If you enjoy sports, think of two sports that have similarities or differences. If you are interested in art, compare and contrast two artists or painting styles.

If you are asked to write a persuasive essay, think about your opinion on the subject. Do you agree or disagree with the issue? What evidence do you have to support your opinion?

When you are brainstorming, do not worry about whether your ideas are good or bad. At this point of the writing process, you just want to create a list of everything you know about a subject and jot down any question you may have about it.

Skills Tip

Make sure you know who your audience is. Your audience will determine the kind of examples you use in your essay, as well as your vocabulary and sentence structure. Writing for peers or classmates is different from writing for professionals or a business.

Organizing Your Ideas

Some writers use clusters, Venn diagrams, or other graphic organizers during brainstorming. The type of essay that you are writing will often determine the kind of organizer that works best.

Examples of Organizing Tools

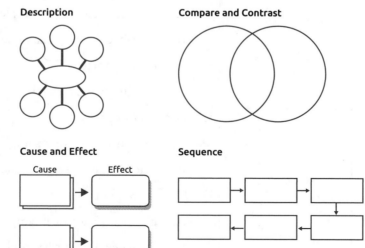

Description

Compare and Contrast

Cause and Effect

Cause   Effect

Sequence

129

Arranging Ideas

Before you outline your prewriting ideas and start writing, there are several ways to order your ideas.

Type	What It Means	When to Use It
Chronological Order	Order events in time order	Historical essays, process essays, recipes, manuals
Importance	Order information beginning with the least importance to most important or vice versa	Explanatory essays, persuasive essays
Logical	Order ideas that relate	Compare-and-contrast essays, cause-and-effect essays, problem-and-solution essays

Planning Your Writing

Once you have brainstormed your ideas and organized them, it is time to plan your essay. All essays need an introduction, a middle (or body), and a conclusion. In the **introduction**, the writer tells the reader what the essay is about. The **body** of the essay provides the readers with facts, descriptions, or examples. The **conclusion** may summarize the main points, provide a solution, or call the reader to action.

Some writers use outlines. Your outline can be formal, complete with Roman numerals and letters, or it can be informal, a simple list of your ideas.

Formal Outline	
	I. Thesis Statement
	II. General Support 1
	A. Evidence, Fact, or Example
	B. Evidence, Fact, or Example
	1. Supporting Detail
	2. Supporting Detail
	III. General Support 2
	A. Evidence, Fact, or Example
	B. Evidence, Fact, or Example
	IV. General Support 3
	A. Evidence, Fact, or Example
	B. Evidence, Fact, or Example
	V. Conclusion

Skills Tip

The tone of your essay may be formal or relaxed, humorous or outraged. Your audience will help you determine the correct tone to use. Your point of view about the topic also sets the tone, but remember, most expository essays should maintain an objective tone. Being objective means being balanced and fair, but it does not mean the writing should be uninteresting!

Informal Outline

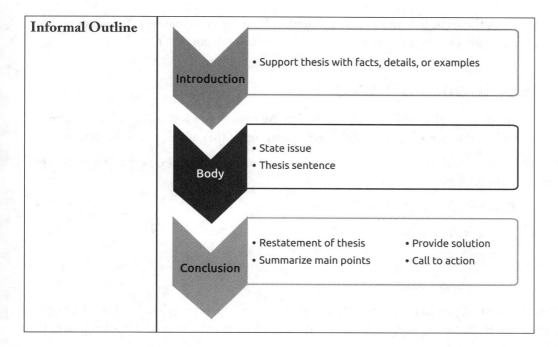

Introduction
- Support thesis with facts, details, or examples

Body
- State issue
- Thesis sentence

Conclusion
- Restatement of thesis
- Summarize main points
- Provide solution
- Call to action

Unit 6 Lesson 2   # LESSON REVIEW

Complete the activity below to check your understanding of the lesson content. The Unit 6 Answer Key is on page 156.

Comprehension

Choose a word from the word bank to complete each sentence.

brainstorming	chronological order	introduction	body	conclusion
outlining	logical order	clustering	audience	tone

1. An essay about the Revolutionary War would *best* be written using _____.

2. A(n) _____ may include a summary or a call to action.

3. An essay that compares zebras and horses would *best* be written using _____.

4. _____ is an activity that allows writers to choose a topic.

5. A writer should consider the _____ when determining the tone of an essay.

6. Supporting details are covered in the _____ of an expository essay.

7. A writer's viewpoint is often expressed by his or her _____.

WRITING THE ROUGH DRAFT

Key Terms

body paragraph

conclusion

formal

informal

introduction

transition

Presenting the right information in the right order in an essay can help to engage your readers, avoid confusing them, and win them over to your point of view.

Developing a Topic

If you have made an outline, you know what information you want to share. Now turn your outline into sentences and build **body paragraphs** that all have topic sentences.

Imagine you are writing an essay about the geography of Mars. This is the first section of your outline:

1. Why is Mars called the Red Planet?

    a. soil

    b. dust storms

    c. rocky surface

In this section, you have one main heading and three supporting details. This is enough for a whole paragraph if you devote a sentence or two to each of your supporting details.

First, introduce your paragraph with a topic sentence:

Mars is also known as the "Red Planet."

Then, explain each of your supporting details:

This is because the soil on the planet contains iron oxide. Iron oxide is another name for rust. Mars also has a ton of dust storms. They last forever and can cover, like, the whole planet. They contribute to the reddish, hazy color of the planet's skies. The landscape of Mars is very rocky. Scientists think the surface of the planet has changed over time like Earth's has. The planet's surface has been affected by lots of events like volcanic eruptions, dust storms, and collisions with other bodies (like meteorites or stars).

This paragraph has covered everything in this section of the outline. Now do the same for the other sections.

Grouping Related Information

As you write, group related information together in the same paragraph. Perhaps you have a sub-point in your outline describing the canyons of Mars. You might move this section to the paragraph about Mars' mountains so that you can discuss these features together.

On the other hand, maybe you have enough information about a volcano on Mars that it can be given its own paragraph. Decide what to emphasize, and then group your facts accordingly.

Skills Tip

Try to write quickly, turning your outline points and supporting details into sentences. Don't worry too much about making your sentences beautiful at this point. Just communicate the information you need to. Then you can go back and decide what needs more attention.

Formal and Informal Language

In your paragraphs, use **formal**, not **informal,** language. An essay is generally written for a business or academic audience, so it should have a formal tone—not the casual language you would use to send an email or a text to a friend.

A formal tone will include:

- more professional language (*Audiences should consider,* rather than *You should think about*)

- more sophisticated vocabulary (*understand* rather than *get*)

- third-person language (avoiding *I* and *my*)

- more specific details

- full words, not contractions (*cannot* rather than *can't*)

Consider this part of the body paragraph about Mars:

> Mars also has a ton of dust storms. They last forever and can cover, like, the whole planet.

Revise these sentences to give them a more formal tone:

> The planet also has frequent dust storms. They last for months and can cover the entire planet.

The informal phrase *a ton of* becomes the more formal *frequent; for months* is more specific and accurate than *forever;* and the slang term *like* has been removed. These sentences now sound more formal.

Introducing Your Topic

Imagine starting your essay with the body paragraph on page 132. Your audience will wonder: *What is this essay about? What is the point?* To avoid confusion, include a good introduction at the beginning that will interest readers in the essay.

An introductory paragraph describes the topic and gives readers a general sense of what will be discussed.

An **introduction** for the essay outlined above might

- start with a generalization: *Mars is one of the most fascinating planets in our solar system.*

- then, explain what *this* essay will discuss: *And while many people may think of the planet as the stuff of science fiction, scientists are busy trying to decipher the geography of the planet.*

- finally, interest your audience in reading more by suggesting what else will be included: *And certainly one of the things scientists are learning is that almost everything is bigger on Mars.*

Transitions

Make relationships between ideas clear through **transitions**: words and phrases that show how paragraphs and sentences relate.

A transition can

- compare two ideas: ***Like*** *pogo sticks, bicycles are human-powered machines.*

- show differences: ***However, unlike*** *pogo sticks, bicycles use wheel-based technology.*

- draw a conclusion: ***Because*** *bicycles do not require the advanced balance skills of pogo sticks, they are a superior form of transportation.*

Concluding Your Essay

To end your essay, provide a **conclusion**—a final paragraph summarizing the essay:

> In conclusion, Mars has fascinating geography. From sand dunes to giant volcanoes, Mars' geographic features offer scientists endless possibilities for research. And the more scientists learn about Mars, the more they hope to unlock secrets about the Earth's past as well.

This conclusion reminds readers what they have read, summarizes the main points, and draws one final conclusion for readers.

Complete the activities below to check your understanding of the lesson content. The Unit 6 Answer Key is on page 156.

Vocabulary

Write a definition in your own words for each of the key terms.

1. body paragraph _____

   _____

2. conclusion _____

   _____

3. introduction _____

   _____

4. transition _____

   _____

Skills Practice

Identify each sentence as having a formal or informal tone.

5. In conclusion, the loss of wildlife habitat in the Great Plains is a problem of increasing urgency.

   _____

6. I think you should get that protecting Antarctica is really important. _____

7. Remember, if you see a news story on TV, there are probably a bunch of things it doesn't mention that a newspaper story probably would. _____

8. Despite his short answer, Benjamin did seem interested in the subject. _____

REVISING AND PROOFREADING

Key Terms

final draft

proofread

revise

slang

Skills Tip

Many essays are written on computer programs that have built-in spell check features. Although running this feature is a good idea, you should still spell check your work with your own eyes as an additional step. This is because sometimes when writing, you can misspell a word as another actual word:

The girl got up from the couch and went too the door.

Here, the writer intended to write *to the door*, but misspelled *to*. Spell check will not know this is wrong, however, because *too* is a real word—just not the one the writer meant!

So, use spell check, but then also check your work yourself. Only you know what you meant to write.

Sometimes, you will need to write and revise several drafts to get your essay ready for proofreading. Once the draft of your essay is written and you are happy with its ideas and organization, it is time to edit it into one final version. This stage will clean up the essay so that it looks polished and professional.

Revising

When you **revise** an essay, you alter your draft to make it better. Think of revising as "re-envisioning" your draft, or seeing it in a new way. Read your essay aloud to yourself or someone else. Ask yourself the following questions:

- How could I make my introductory paragraph more interesting?
- What details and examples could I add to clarify my ideas?
- Are the paragraphs organized logically?
- Did I include transitions from one paragraph to another?
- Are there words I could replace with stronger or more precise words?
- Is there anything that should be taken out because it does not support my main idea?

Check Your Logic

As you revise, check your essay for logic. Make sure that each sentence follows naturally from the one before it.

If a sentence does not flow naturally, determine why:

- If it is unrelated to the paragraph it is in, move it to a new place where it fits better.
- If it is unrelated to anything else in the essay, eliminate it.
- If it just needs more clarity, add a transition.

For instance, in this paragraph:

Some of Shakespeare's plays were not printed until many years after his death. The possibility always exists that we could still find another we do not yet know about!

The relationship between the two sentences is not totally clear. Adding the word *Therefore* at the beginning of the second sentence will make the relationship much clearer:

Some of Shakespeare's plays were not printed until many years after his death. Therefore, the possibility always exists that we could still find another we do not yet know about!

Proofreading a Final Draft

The final step in writing an essay is to create a **final draft** that will be submitted as finished and complete. To create the final draft, you must **proofread** your essay: read it carefully to check for any unintentional errors, such as:

- spelling mistakes

- incorrect verb tense

- incorrect punctuation

- informal language

You are not looking at the essay's *ideas*, which should already be as you want them. Instead, you are assessing its *language*.

Different people have different strategies for proofreading. Some choose to refer to a list of error types (like grammar, spelling, and transitions) and check for all errors at once. Others read their work once for spelling, then read it again for grammar. Still other people read their essays backward, one sentence at a time, so that they can focus on each sentence as it was written.

Use the strategy that works best for you.

Spoken and Written Language

The language we use in everyday speech is different from the language of a formal essay. You might say to a friend:

> *Dude, I totally thought the main guy in the film seemed like kind of a jerk.*

This is fine—in informal spoken language. In an essay, formal language is the rule:

> *The main character appears mean-spirited.*

In an essay, use formal written language, not spoken language. This means

- eliminating any first-person point of view (words like *I*, *me*, *my*).

- spelling out words rather than using contractions (*will not* rather than *won't*).

- being specific (*several minutes* rather than *a while*).

- using a more sophisticated vocabulary (*understand* rather than *get it*).

Eliminate Slang

Eliminate from your essay any traces of **slang**, or very informal or casual language that you would use in speech but not in writing. This includes words like *hey*, *awesome*, and *how come*.

Slang that should be eliminated includes words specific to your region. For instance, the expression *y'all*, if you use it in speech, should become *you* in an essay. Your goal is to be easily understood by anyone who reads your essay, regardless of background.

Final Steps

As a final step, check your punctuation. Are any titles in the essay italicized, underlined, or in quotation marks, depending on the type of title? Did you end all questions with a question mark?

Once this is done, congratulations! Your essay is complete.

Complete the activities below to check your understanding of the lesson content. The Unit 6 Answer Key is on page 156.

Vocabulary

Write a definition in your own words for each of the key terms.

1. final draft _____

_____

2. proofreading _____

_____

3. slang _____

_____

Skills Practice

Proofread these sentences as if they were part of a formal essay. Make any corrections on the lines below.

4. Jaime was all to his friend, "Hey man, how's it going?"

_____

_____

5. Yesterday, she studies the book throughly for clues to the mysterie.

_____

_____

6. After their run, she was like, "I'm beat."

_____

_____

7. The dog came across as very agressive.

_____

_____

Answer the questions based on the content covered in this unit. The Unit 6 Answer Key is on page 157.

Use the following paragraph to answer questions 1–6.

To the Editor,

I recently read that the city is planning to cut back on the number of bike lanes on the city streets. I am a student who rides a bike. Like many others, I use my bicycle for different things: I ride my bike to school, I ride to run errands, and I ride because it is fun. Bike lanes are often the only "roads" that keep bike riders safe. Bike lanes clearly mark where bike riders are supposed to ride their bikes. They also help drivers be clear about their lanes, too. Taking away the bike lanes will increase the risk of accidents.

1. What type of expository essay is this?

   A. explanatory

   B. informative

   C. persuasive

   D. informal

2. Which of the following details expresses the writer's tone?

   A. "the city is planning to cut back on the number of bike lanes"

   B. "I ride my bike to school"

   C. "I ride because it is fun"

   D. "increase the risk of accidents"

3. Which of the following sentences would *best* end the essay?

   A. The city council members are wrong, and I insist that they reconsider their plans.

   B. Rather than reducing the number of bike lanes, for safety's sake, we should be expanding the number of bike lanes.

   C. Getting rid of bike lanes is a huge waste of money.

   D. Anyone who rides a bike knows how dangerous the streets can be, so let's keep our city bike friendly.

4. The writer's position is that she (supports, opposes) the plan about cutting back on the number of bike lanes.

5. The writer supports her essay using (logical, emotional) appeals.

6. Complete the diagram using details from the essay.

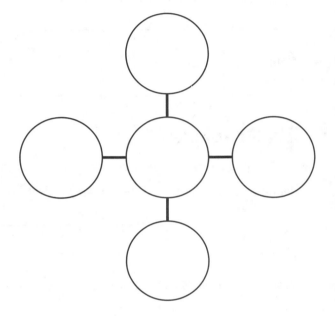

Write your response on the line provided.

7. What are the four steps of the writing process?

   _____

   _____

   _____

   _____

8. What is the best way to organize an essay about a historical event?

   _____

   _____

Revise the underlined words in each sentence on the following lines to give the sentence a more formal tone.

9. She is certain there is a solution, but she <u>doesn't get how to come up with</u> it.

   _____

10. <u>Lots of folks</u> are in the same situation as Steve.

    _____

11. There is reason to be optimistic <u>when you look at it that way</u>.

    _____

12. <u>It's pretty obvious</u> that we already have the answer to our question.

    _____

Choose the appropriate transition for the blank.

On the other hand	Therefore
Similarly	Otherwise

13. Sea temperatures are rising, and many fish species are dying off. _____, we must make a concerted effort to find a solution.

14. One presidential candidate makes excellent points about the economy. _____, I prefer her opponent's views on the military.

15. The large canyon reflects a meteor bombardment from many thousands of years ago. _____, the smaller one nearby also resulted from space debris.

16. With focused attention to diplomacy, the two countries may find a peaceful solution to their conflict. _____, they may be looking at a violent future.

Underline the slang words that should be replaced in a formal essay.

17. Man, she flipped out when she heard about their argument.

18. He was blown away by her act of kindness and thought, "She's awesome."

19. The players thought they had the game in the bag, but check this, the score was still up for grabs in the eighth inning.

Underline the spelling errors in the following sentences.

20. The child's arguement was completly effective, and she did end up receiving ice cream.

21. Petra seemed to be acting wierd, but it turned out that she was just embarassed.

22. After months of saying we would meet up, we finaly put it on the calender.

Answer these questions to see how well you have learned the reading and writing content and skills in this book.

Read the following passage, and then answer questions 1–11.

A Civil War Soldier Named Olive

After supper, Olive Richards performed her usual chores. She cleared the table and helped her mother wash and dry dishes. Uncle Joe, too old to be drafted, who was staying with Olive's family while her father was off in battle, retired to the front porch with the newspaper. Olive's little sister Judith went off to attend to her schoolwork. At the sink in her apron, her mother sighed only a few times.

They functioned like a family now, with Uncle Joe in place of Father. A family still, just a smaller family. All their interactions were colored with the strained courtesy of the bravely beleaguered. Each of them was thinking of Mr. Richards (their father, their husband, their brother) and Olive's brother, Todd, only 17. They spoke of the endangered men as little as possible, each to spare the other of additional worry. But each of them, once a week or so, broke down and made a tearful outburst before regaining strength to go on running the farm as if everything were normal. Milking at dawn, gathering eggs, cooking for the women; Uncle Joe threshing grain and feeding the livestock. They rationed their goods and their energies.

Olive had told no one of her secret plan to escape the torturous feeling of helplessness.

The kitchen tidy, Olive went to Judith's room, kissed her sister's cheek, and said, "Study hard, Sis." Judith threw her an appreciative but perplexed look as the lantern light flicked golden on her innocent face.

For a few minutes, Olive sat on her bed in silence, her hands in her lap, a look of fright on her face that shifted slowly into determination. She knew from Todd's letters that conditions in the Army were trying. It was cold and muddy. Every day soldiers died from diseases like influenza or dysentery, or infections from battle wounds. She knew it was a place of hardship and strain that tested a soldier's faith and resolve. But she also knew it strengthened one's patriotism and fulfilled something that could not be fulfilled otherwise: a sense of duty to protect what you valued.

Todd's initial days after enlisting were filled with drills broken by an occasional stint at guard duty and interminable waiting. Then at last the orders came to march. Olive could only hope that her wait would be short and that, at camp among the boys and men, her real identity would not betray her.

Finally, she arose from bed, and seeing that the sun had sunk below the alfalfa field, Olive excused herself to the barn on a false errand, nearly detected by her ever-wary mother. There, in an empty horse stall, Olive hacked her hair with a penknife and pulled on a bulky jacket and wool pants she'd fashioned herself from a blanket. Finally, she smeared dirt on her face. Her image in a dusty mirror confirmed that the transformation was complete. No one would be able to tell that this was not a rugged young man heading off to volunteer in the War of Rebellion. No one would be able to tell that she was a woman.

Olive's family would've been shocked at her audacity, but she was determined to fight for the Union and for the end of slavery. The physical exam worried Olive, but she had heard Uncle Joe saying to a farmhand that the rush to move men to the battlefield was so hurried that army physicians made only a perfunctory check that a solider had all his teeth and could hold a musket. Before the mirror, she adjusted her shoulders into their ultimate bulk and practiced her manly stroll. After that, Olive deepened her voice and said confidently, "Albert. Albert Johnson. I come up from Muiresville. I'd rather be playing baseball, but I figured to pitch in for the cause."

Nellie, the family mule, snuffled from the neighboring stall as if to laugh at her impression.

Olive gathered the sack of provisions she'd stashed and stepped out onto the road, turned muddy by recent rain. With the moon rising, she set out into the night toward the battlefront. She was unaware that she was one of about 400 Union and Confederate women who disguised themselves as men to fight in the Civil War.

1. Which clue from the passage helps the reader to identify the setting?

   A. "fight for the Union and for the end of slavery"

   B. "Olive Richards performed her usual chores"

   C. "Olive gathered the sack of provisions"

   D. "'I figured to pitch in for the cause'"

2. What types of clues offer hints about a story's setting?

   A. the use of technology

   B. the geography

   C. the weather

   D. all of the above

Write your responses on the lines provided.

3. What is the point of view of "A Civil War Soldier Named Olive"?

   _____

   _____

4. Identify three words or phrases from the passage that help you to determine the point of view of the story.

   _____

   _____

5. What phrases from the passage indicate direct characterization?

   _____

   _____

6. What type(s) of external conflict does Olive experience in "A Civil War Soldier Named Olive"?

   _____

   _____

7. What type(s) of internal conflict does Olive experience in "A Civil War Soldier Named Olive"?

   _____

   _____

8. At what point does the rising action begin in "A Civil War Soldier Named Olive"?

   A. "They functioned like a family now"

   B. "Olive had told no one of her secret plan"

   C. "Olive sat on her bed in silence"

   D. "Finally, she arose from the bed"

9. What is the denouement of "A Civil War Soldier Named Olive"?

   A. Olive's family was in shock.

   B. Women from both the Union and the Confederacy disguised themselves as men to fight.

   C. Olive had to deepen her voice to be convincing.

   D. Olive changed her name to Albert Johnson.

10. What is the theme of "A Civil War Soldier Named Olive"?

   A. Women have historically overcome fear and societal limitations to fight for what they believe in.

   B. Women and men should have an equal opportunity to defend their country.

   C. Olive's mother plans to protect Olive by keeping her at home.

   D. Olive plans to fight in the Civil War.

11. Which of the following details helps to reveal the writer's tone?

   A. "Olive's little sister Judith went off to attend to her schoolwork."

   B. "Todd's initial days after enlisting were filled with drills broken by an occasional stint at guard duty and interminable waiting."

   C. "But she also knew it strengthened one's patriotism and fulfilled something that could not be fulfilled otherwise: a sense of duty to protect what you valued."

   D. "No one would be able to tell that she was a woman."

Read the following poem, and then answer questions 12–16.

Reflection

Gull songs on a lazy afternoon,
A young girl in a bright yellow dress
fishes off a pier,
beaming like the sun.

She is a mirror to my past,
to what I have forgotten.
I breathe in the salty mist;
rhythmic waves begin to erase time.

As light fades, the sunset brushes the sky,
Setting the horizon on fire,
pink, purple, and gold.
Memories flow swiftly.

12. Which of the following lines is the best example of personification?

   A. "Gull songs on a lazy afternoon"

   B. "She is a mirror to my past"

   C. "I breathe in the salty mist"

   D. "As light fades, the sunset brushes the sky"

13. What feature of the coastal scene is NOT important to the speaker?

   A. its color   C. its vastness

   B. its sounds   D. its quietness

14. The poem suggests that people

   A. regret the choices that they have made.

   B. should cherish each living moment.

   C. need to find a balance with nature.

   D. attach too much importance to youth.

15. The speaker states that the young girl was "beaming like the sun" and that she "is a mirror to my past / to what I have forgotten." Explain what you think the speaker means. Support your answer with details from the poem.

   _____

   _____

   _____

16. The poet includes several colors in the poem—the yellow dress and the pink, purple, and gold sunset. What might these colors symbolize? What might the sunset symbolize?

   _____

   _____

   _____

Read the following passage, and then answer questions 17–19.

Setting: A country kitchen. Helen is sitting at a table, center stage, reading a newspaper, drinking coffee. Cody enters the stage, stretching his arms and yawning.

Cody: The house is so quiet this morning! Where are the kids? Have you all eaten breakfast?

Helen: *(still reading the newspaper)* It will stay quiet if you lower your voice. *(She looks up.)* Coffee is ready, and I was thinking of making pancakes when the kids wake up. They're Molly's favorite . . . and since it's her birthday. Did you pick up the bike? I didn't see it.

Cody: *(Pours coffee and smacks his forehead.)* Is that today? Wow! I thought that was next week. I'll run into town this afternoon. Wilson's Sporting has plenty of bikes. Don't worry.

Molly, a ten-year-old girl, enters the room, still in pajamas.

Molly: Did I hear something about pancakes and a bike? *(She grins and hugs her dad.)*

Helen: *(Squints her eyes at Cody.)* Good morning, birthday girl! *(She stands and kisses Molly on the head.)* I said I would make pancakes and that later we could go for a *hike*. Now, go wake up your brother so that we can have those pancakes. *(Helen scoots Molly out of the kitchen and wags her finger at Cody.)* Geez, do you know how to whisper? And you better hope Wilson's has children's bikes. You know how long Molly has been asking for a bike.

17. Which event will most likely create a conflict between the characters?

   A. Cody goes into town to buy Molly's bike.

   B. Helen makes pancakes for breakfast.

   C. Molly tries to wake up her brother.

   D. Wilson's does not have a bike for Molly.

18. What character trait does the audience learn about Cody from this scene?

    A. He is forgetful.

    B. He is a caring father.

    C. He enjoys birthday parties.

    D. He enjoys going on hikes.

19. Explain how the stage directions and dialogue show how Helen tries to keep Molly's present a surprise. What does this action reveal about Helen?

    _____

    _____

    _____

Read the following passage, and then answer questions 20–27.

America's Super Trail: The Appalachian Trail

In 1925, Benton MacKaye, a planner for the U.S. Forest Service, had a vision. He believed the United States needed a "super trail." MacKaye believed that this footpath would offer Americans an escape from modern life. It would
[5]   provide recreation and would include camp shelters and wilderness communities. MacKaye's vision was never fully realized. However, it came close in the form of the 2,175-mile route known as the Appalachian Trail.

Today, the Appalachian National Scenic Trail is the nation's
[10] longest marked footpath, stretching from Georgia to Maine. Its acreage is all public land. The trail cuts through 14 states, with heights ranging from 124 feet to a staggering 6,625 feet above sea level. Campgrounds and shelters aid hikers along the route. A number of towns along the trail are also
[15] known for their hospitality toward hikers. In between, hikers can enjoy spectacular landscapes that showcase the diverse flora and fauna found in the eastern United States.

The trail's construction began in New York in 1923 and was finally completed in 1937. Volunteer groups, as well
[20] as the Civilian Conservation Corps, made the trail and its support buildings. With the outbreak of World War II, the trail fell into disrepair. However, volunteers again came to the trail's rescue. By 1951, the trail was restored.

The trail attracts hikers from all over the world. Most will
[25] attempt only short sections of the trail over the course of one or two days. However, there are others who aim higher by

hiking the entire trail, which requires almost 5 million steps! Each year, approximately 500 hikers successfully complete the hike, which can take anywhere from 5 to 7 months.

20. What is the purpose of this passage?

    A. to inform the reader about how the Appalachian Trail was built

    B. to entertain the reader with a story about the Appalachian Trail

    C. to encourage the reader to hike on the Appalachian Trail

    D. to persuade the reader to learn more about the Appalachian Trail

21. The campgrounds and shelters along the Appalachian Trail were placed there to

    A. provide jobs for people who live along the trail.

    B. show hikers the correct route to follow.

    C. showcase the unique wilderness landscape.

    D. help hikers as they move along the trail.

22. As it is used in this passage, *hospitality* (line 15) most nearly means

    A. friendliness.   C. uncertainty.

    B. safety.   D. medical care.

23. Based on the information in the passage, most people who hike the Appalachian Trail

    A. hike the entire length of the trail.

    B. spend only a day or two hiking.

    C. take 5 million steps.

    D. do not use the shelters provided.

24. This passage is most likely to be found in a

    A. biography of a hiker.

    B. local newspaper.

    C. history textbook.

    D. scientific journal.

25. Write a sentence describing the main idea of the passage.

    _____

    _____

26. What is the topic sentence in paragraph 2?

    _____

    _____

27. Based on the information in the passage, why did Benton MacKaye want to build a "super trail"?

    _____

    _____

28. <u>Peter</u> and <u>Maria</u> took their <u>cats</u> to the veterinarian's <u>office</u> after <u>school</u>. The underlined words in this sentence are

    A. nouns.

    B. pronouns.

    C. verbs.

    D. adjectives.

29. Which of the following correctly completes this sentence?

    We will _____ into our new house in August.

    A. moved

    B. be moving

    C. did move

    D. moving

30. Which of the following shows the best way to combine these two sentences?

    David is a cook. He volunteers at the high school teaching students how to bake.

    A. David, who is a cook, volunteers at the high school teaching students how to bake.

    B. David is a cook and David volunteers at the high school teaching students how to bake.

    C. David, volunteers at the high school teaching students how to bake, is a cook.

    D. David volunteers at the high school teaching students how to bake, but he is also a cook.

31. Which of the following correctly completes this sentence?

    All three of my sisters meet at the track and _____ together three times a week.

    A. ran

    B. run

    C. runs

    D. will run

32. Which of the following is the best correction of the underlined portion of these sentences?

    I have to get to bed early tonight. Because I have an appointment first thing in the morning.

    A. No change needed.

    B. tonight; because

    C. tonight because

    D. tonight—because

33. Rewrite this sentence with correct punctuation.

    I asked my boss if I could buy lemonade chips and sandwiches for our lunch meeting.

    _____

    _____

34. Correct the spelling error in this sentence.

    Our office is currently excepting applications for all positions.

    _____

35. Correct the capitalization error in this sentence.

    Center City community college is holding auditions for its annual play this Saturday.

    _____

36. What pronoun is needed to complete this sentence?

    My brother and I are both applying for a job at the restaurant on our street; I hope _____ are both hired.

    _____

37. What adverb is needed to complete this sentence?

    Students should proceed to the auditorium
    _____ they have signed in.

    _____

38. Match each of the following terms to its correct definition.

introduction	continuation of the events after the climax that ends the story
conflict	turning point of the conflict
rising action	the main body of the story that continues the development of the conflict
climax	the conclusion of the story
falling action	establishes the setting and characters
denouement	when two opposing forces meet

39. Explain the difference between direct and indirect characterization.

    _____

    _____

    _____

    _____

40. Explain in one or two sentences the difference between internal and external conflict.

    _____

    _____

    _____

    _____

41. What is the difference between third-person limited and third-person omniscient points of view?

    _____

    _____

    _____

42. Which of the following is NOT a definition of *theme*?

    A. the central concept that makes a statement about the topic

    B. an expression of the writer's opinion

    C. a general message the writer is trying to convey about life

    D. a listing of the series of events that make up the rising and falling action

Read the following passage, and then answer questions 43–46.

[1] The first Olympics, as early as 776 BCE, invited participants from across the Greek world. [2] Every four years, people would travel to compete and celebrate athletics. [3] Warring regions had to accept a Sacred Truce. [4] This truce allowed people to travel peacefully and enjoy the events together. [5] Today, the modern Olympics carry out this ancient vision.

43. Which topic sentence would be most appropriate for this paragraph?

    A. The Olympics have a long history associated with ancient Greece.

    B. The Olympic Games have always encouraged peace across cultures.

    C. Archaeologists claim humans have competed in sports for as long as they can identify.

    D. The latest Olympic Games were the most popular athletic competition in history.

44. Which sentence contains a supporting detail?

    A. 1   C. 4

    B. 3   D. 5

45. Which transition phrase most effectively introduces sentence 3?

    A. On the other hand,   C. In conclusion,

    B. Even so,   D. Thus,

46. Which sentence, if added after sentence 5, would offer the best supporting details for sentence 5?

   A. Today, both the summer and winter Olympics are watched on television the world over, with viewers in nearly two hundred countries.

   B. The athletic events of the Olympics have changed dramatically since the first Games— not to mention, athletes now compete wearing clothes.

   C. Swimming is currently the most popular and widely viewed of all the summer Olympic contests, and the summer Games in general are more popular than the winter Games.

   D. The Olympics are a powerful opportunity for nations to set aside differences and conflict to gather and celebrate the human capacity for skill, speed, and strength.

Read the following passage, and then answer questions 47–49.

You will find that school uniforms lead to happiness and less stress for students who wear them. Uniforms have resulted in less pressure on families who may be struggling financially. Other families simply prefer not to waste money on clothes for their quickly growing children. Strict dress codes may result in increased conformity. However, lower-income students feel less pressure to compete, fashion-wise, with their better-off peers. Students will learn to judge each other on their character—not on their ability to keep up with trends. The school district should seriously consider this idea.

47. What is the author's purpose for this paragraph?

   _____

   _____

48. Summarize the main details of the paragraph in your own words.

   _____

   _____

   _____

   _____

49. Based on the details, write a topic sentence that you think best identifies the main idea that the author is addressing.

   _____

   _____

Complete each sentence with the most appropriate transition word or phrase.

50. Stephen did an award-winning science project this year. _____, he delivered a highly commended speech in the debate tournament.

   A. Therefore   C. In addition

   B. As a result   D. Even so

51. We have many reasons to recommend him for the job. _____, it will entail a lot more responsibility than he has had in the past.

   A. On the other hand C. Thus

   B. In addition   D. In conclusion

52. Yanick is always willing to help out a friend. _____, he spent all last weekend aiding Sarah with her history presentation.

   A. Nevertheless   C. In addition

   B. For example   D. Yet

Choose a word from the word bank to complete each sentence.

expository	body	logical
persuasive	proofread	conclusion
outline	transition	final draft

53. A writer makes final corrections to grammar and spelling in order to produce a

   _____.

54. A(n) _____ essay tries to win the audience to its point of view.

55. A writer should _____ for any errors before submitting an essay.

56. A(n) _____ paragraph includes the main details of an essay.

57. A(n) _____ essay explores a topic in depth.

58. A(n) _____ is used to connect ideas within an essay.

59. A writer should make sure his or her ideas flow in a(n) _____ order.

60. Before turning ideas into an essay, organize them by creating a(n) _____.

61. An essay's _____ synthesizes the information it has presented.

Identify each sentence as having a formal or informal tone.

62. In addition, the decline in quality in American infrastructure is an issue of increasing importance.

_____

63. It's like the whole world is into the idea of video games these days. _____

64. Despite her lingering doubts, she ultimately chose to take the job as a way of proving her skills.

_____

Read the following passage, and then answer questions 65–67.

[1] Dinesen went to school at the Academy of Fine Arts in Copenhagen and later married her second-cousin, Baron Bror Blixen-Finecke. [2] In 1914, they went together to British East Africa, known today as Kenya, where they owned a farm. [3] At first they were going to raise cattle, but then they went, 'No let's grow and harvest coffee instead.' [4] They enjoyed big game hunting and a close relationship with the native tribespeople, called Kikuyu.

65. What type of essay is this?

A. investigative

B. persuasive

C. expository

D. informal

66. Which sentence should be rewritten to give it a more formal tone?

A. 1   C. 3

B. 2   D. 4

67. Which sentence offers the best introduction to this paragraph?

A. Many Europeans made a living in the early twentieth century running plantations in Africa.

B. Many women have historically chosen to write and publish under male pennames.

C. The writer Isak Dinesen, author of *Out of Africa*, is the penname, or *nom de plume*, of Karen Christence Dinesen, a Danish woman born August 17, 1885.

D. Although many people associate African agriculture with coffee, the cattle trade is quite large as well.

Put the steps of the writing process in order.

68. Revising   Prewriting   Proofreading   Drafting

_____

_____

Correct the spelling errors in the following sentences.

69. We had prepared for bad weather, but it actualy turned out to be beautiful that afternoon.

_____

_____

70. We were estonished that he thought he could cheat so obviously and get away with it.

_____

_____

71. After submitting several drafts, Jaime's essay was pronounced acceptible.

_____

_____

POSTTEST ANSWER KEY

1. **A.** Choice A indicates the location and time.

2. **D.** Since setting is the time and place of a story, all choices are correct.

3. **third-person limited** Third-person limited is correct because the narrator does not divulge the thoughts of other characters.

4. **Possible answers:** "Olive Richards performed her usual chores," "Olive went to Judith's room," "She knew from Todd's letters." Each of these sentences contains details based on Olive's knowledge.

5. **Possible answers:** "a look of fright on her face that shifted slowly into determination," "determined to fight for the Union," and "confidently." The narrator tells the reader directly how Olive feels: "a look of fright on her face that shifted slowly into determination."

6. **Character against character:** Olive vs. her mother; **Character against society:** Olive vs. traditional roles of women at that time.

7. **Character against her conscience:** Olive's sense of duty vs. her fear; **Character against her wants/needs:** Olive wants to overcome her feeling of helplessness and fulfill her sense of duty.

8. **B.** "Olive had told no one of her secret plan" concludes the introduction and indicates action and conflict to come.

9. **B.** The resolution of the story is when the reader is told that Olive was not the only woman to go to war disguised as a man.

10. **A.** Choice B is a moral. Choice C is one subject of the story. Choice D is a plot summary.

11. **C.** Since tone is the attitude of the author, only choice C is an example of the author's feelings.

12. **D.** This question asks that you identify personification—a literary device that gives inanimate objects human-like qualities. The sunset brushing the sky gives the sunset arms, like an artist using a brush to paint the sky.

13. **D.** This question asks you to evaluate the imagery the poet uses. The speaker addresses the color, sounds, and vastness of the setting sun on a coastal scene but does not mention the scene as being quiet.

14. **B.** This question asks that you state the theme of the poem. The poet reveals that people grow old quickly and soon forget their youth. The imagery suggests that people should slow down and appreciate each moment.

15. **Possible answer:** The speaker sees that the girl is happy. She is young, carefree, and full of life. The image of the girl reminds the speaker of her past. The girl is reflecting what the speaker used to look like. The speaker has forgotten to enjoy life—forgotten how to fish and relax. When the speaker does relax, her childhood memories come back. This question asks that you explain the simile, "beaming like the sun" and the metaphor "she is a mirror to my past / to what I have forgotten." When the speaker sees the girl, she notices the young girl's happiness. The image of the girl reminds the speaker of her past.

16. **Possible answer:** The yellow dress represents the youth of the speaker— her childhood. As she ages, the color turns to pinks and purple. These colors represent growing older. The youthful bright yellow fades to a gold color, representing the golden years. The colors and the sunset symbolize the speaker's growing older. This question asks that you explain the symbolism of the colors. Color symbolism is often culturally based; the sample answer is based on the commonly accepted meanings of colors in the United States.

17. **D.** This question asks you to infer what the conflict will be, based on the dialogue. Cody has forgotten the bike, and this has already caused conflict between him and Helen. Readers can infer that if the sporting goods store does not have a suitable bike for Molly, this will cause a conflict between Cody and Helen and between Molly and her parents.

18. **A.** This question asks that you analyze the character based on stage directions and dialogue. The text supports the idea that Cody is forgetful. He did not remember Molly's birthday, and he forgot to buy her bike.

19. **Possible answer:** Helen tries to distract Molly by kissing her and sending Molly to wake her brother. In her dialogue, she tries to convince Molly she misunderstood her parents' conversation by saying she and Cody were talking about a hike, not a bike. Her actions and words show that Helen loves her daughter and wants to make this a special day for Molly. This question asks that you analyze the character based on stage directions and dialogue.

20. **A.** The passage is informative and has a neutral tone. Choice A best describes the purpose.

21. **D.** Paragraph 2 describes how the shelters support the trail by "aiding" hikers.

22. **A.** The context clues demonstrate that the towns are friendly toward the hikers.

23. **B.** The final paragraph states that most hikers only spend a short time on the trail.

24. **C.** The passage gives an informative overview of the trail. The tone is neutral and objective, like that of a history textbook.

25. **Possible answer:** The Appalachian Trail is a popular U.S. trail that offers an incredible experience to hikers. Correct answers will note that the "super trail" is a popular trail in the United States.

26. **Today, the Appalachian National Scenic Trail is the nation's longest marked footpath, stretching from Georgia to Maine.** The rest of the paragraph supports this topic sentence.

27. **He wanted to build a trail to provide Americans with a place for recreation and an escape from modern life.** Correct answers will note MacKaye's wish for an "escape" from modern life.

28. **A.** The words that are underlined are people, places, and things. These are all nouns.

29. **B.** The verb needs to indicate that the action will happen in the future.

30. **A.** This answer appropriately combines the sentences by adding "who is a cook" as a description of David. This keeps the focus on the primary information, which involves his volunteer work.

31. **B.** The present tense of the verb "meet" at the beginning of the sentence tells you that "run" must also be in present tense. Verb tenses should match or make chronological sense in the sentence.

32. **C.** No punctuation is needed to separate the clause beginning with "because" from the rest of the sentence.

33. **I asked my boss if I could buy lemonade, chips, and sandwiches for our lunch meeting.** This question asks you to separate the items in a list or series. Commas are needed to break up the items in the series.

34. **accepting** This question looks at the commonly confused words *accepting* and *excepting*. *Excepting* means "excluding," but the office is taking applications. *Accepting* is the proper spelling of the word in this instance.

35. **Community College** Center City Community College is a proper noun.

36. **we** "My brother and I" is plural, therefore a plural pronoun is needed. Pronouns must match their antecedent in number.

37. **after** The sentence suggests the students will sign in and then go to the auditorium. "After" correctly indicates this series of events.

38. **introduction**—establishes the setting and characters

    conflict—when two opposing forces meet

    rising action—the main body of the story that continues the development of the conflict

    climax—turning point of the conflict

    falling action—continuation of the events after the climax that ends the story

    denouement—the conclusion of the story

39. Direct characterization is when the narrator tells the reader directly how a character feels and what kind of person the character is. Indirect characterization is when the author provides details about a character's speech, dress, appearance, and actions and the reader must determine what these details mean.

40. External conflict can be between people, against larger natural forces, or against an idea in society. Internal conflict is when the character experiences a problem or struggle within himself or herself.

41. Third-person limited point of view describes, in third person, the thoughts of only one particular character, while a third-person omniscient narrator knows the thoughts of all characters.

42. **D.** A series of events is the definition of *plot*.

43. **B.** The paragraph emphasizes the history of the Olympics bringing people together. Choice B emphasizes this aspect the best.

44. **C.** Sentence 4 provides additional detail about Olympic truces.

45. **D.** Sentence 3 makes a statement that follows from sentence 2. Therefore, "thus" is an appropriate transition word.

46. **D.** Choice D provides specific details about the way the modern Olympics bring together people in a similar fashion to the ancient Olympics.

47. **Possible answer: to persuade the local school district to consider implementing a uniform policy for students.** The paragraph includes reasons school uniforms offer advantages to families and students, and it concludes by suggesting the school district investigate uniforms. Therefore, the purpose seems to be to persuade the school district of the value of uniforms.

48. Answers should reference decreased financial pressure on families and the increased ability of students to see past the superficial aspects of each other's clothes. The details of this paragraph that support its argument are that uniforms save money and reduce disparities between students of different financial means.

49. **Possible answer: This district should implement a school uniform policy because it would offer multiple benefits to students and their parents.** The paragraph seems to be offering an argument in favor of uniforms. A good topic sentence will declare that uniforms are a good idea for this school district.

50. **C.** The sentences emphasize the quantity of Stephen's work; therefore, "in addition" is an appropriate transition.

51. **A.** The second sentence suggests a relationship of opposition; therefore, "on the other hand" is an appropriate transition.

52. **B.** The first sentence identifies a characteristic, and the second provides an example of it; therefore, "for example" is an appropriate transition.

53. **final draft** A final draft is a final, finished piece of writing.

54. **persuasive** A persuasive essay tries to convince an audience of something rather than describing a subject.

55. **proofread** Proofreading involves checking an essay for minor errors in spelling, tone, and grammar.

56. **body** A body paragraph provides details on a subject, unlike an introduction or a conclusion.

57. **expository** An expository essay describes a topic rather than persuading the reader.

58. **transition** A transition connects ideas within an essay.

59. **logical** Details in an essay should connect to each other logically.

60. **outline** An outline helps a writer organize his or her thoughts before drafting.

61. **conclusion** A conclusion brings together all the information an essay has presented.

62. **formal** This sentence has a formal tone, with vocabulary and grammar appropriate to an essay.

63. **informal** This sentence has an informal tone, with its casual word choices of "into" and "it's like."

64. **formal** This sentence has a formal tone, with vocabulary and grammar appropriate to an essay.

65. **C.** This appears to be an expository essay describing a subject's life.

66. **C.** This sentence has an informal tone, because it includes the phrase "then they went" to mean "they decided."

67. **C.** This paragraph appears to be the introduction to a biography; therefore, a general sentence introducing the subject is appropriate.

68. [1] Prewriting is the first step in the writing process.

    [2] Drafting should take place after a writer has prewritten the ideas.

    [3] Revising takes place after drafting is complete.

    [4] Revising is the final step in the writing process.

69. **actualy** The word should be spelled "actually."

70. **estonished** The word should be spelled "astonished."

71. **acceptible** The word should be spelled "acceptable."

POSTTEST ANSWER KEY

After checking your Posttest answers using the Answer Key, use the chart below to find the questions you did not answer correctly. Then locate the pages in this book where you can review the content needed to answer those questions correctly.

Question	Where to Look for Help		
	Unit	Lesson	Page
1, 2	1	1	13
3, 4, 41	1	2	15
5, 39	1	3	18
6, 7, 8, 9, 38, 40	1	4	21
10, 42	1	6	28
11	2	4	44
12	2	3	40
13, 14	2	5	46
15	2	3	40
16	2	2	37
17, 18	2	7	50
19	2	6	48
20, 21, 23, 24	3	1	56
22	3	7	73
25, 26, 43	5	1	115
27, 47, 48, 49	3	2	59
28, 37	4	1	80
29, 36	4	6	99
30, 33	4	4	92
31	4	8	104
32	4	3	88
34	4	9	110
35	4	7	102
44, 46	5	2	118
45	5	3	121
50, 51, 52, 53, 55, 58, 68	6	4	136
54, 57, 65	6	1	125
56, 61, 62, 63, 64, 66, 67	6	3	132
59, 60	6	2	129
69, 70, 71	4	9	108

ANSWER KEY

Unit 1: Reading Fiction Prose

Lesson 1: Setting

1. the time and place a story occurs
2. Answers will vary but should include the idea of outer space or a spaceship. The time should be in the future.
3. Answers will vary but should mention "the planet," "Station 4," "the whole mission," and Cassini, which seems likely to be a spaceship.

Lesson 2: Point of View

1. the perspective from which a story is told
2. the narrator is a character in the story
3. the narrator is telling someone else's story.
4. the narrator knows only one character's thoughts and feelings.
5. the narrator knows the thoughts and feelings of more than one character
6. third-person omniscient
7. Answers may vary but should include a phrase indicating that the narrator has access to the thoughts of multiple characters, e.g., "Kate thought if the judges did not make up their minds…" and "But little did she realize that Tomas and Jonah were as anxious as she."

Lesson 3: Characterization

1. a person or role in a story
2. a character involved heavily in the main plot
3. a character who is less important to the story
4. revealing a character's personality by stating what he or she is like
5. revealing a character's personality by providing details that suggest what he or she is like
6. C.
7. A.
8. B.
9. C.

Lesson 4: Plot

1. the series of events that happen in a story
2. the turning point when the conflict is resolved
3. the conclusion of the story
4. external
5. internal
6. external
7. introduction, rising action, climax, falling action, denouement

Lesson 5: Mood and Tone

1. Mood
2. Tone
3. Tone
4. Mood
5. gloomy
6. loving
7. excited

Lesson 6: Theme

1. A plot summary
2. The theme
3. A moral
4. The theme
5. The theme

Unit Practice Test

1. C. The setting is the Nebraska prairie at a time when cameras had already been invented, so the story must take place over a century ago.
2. A.
3. first person
4. Sample answer: "I was twelve years old, the summer Mr. Butcher came to take our pictures." or "I remember dashing into the yard, tearing off my apron, my mother's disapproving clucks in my ear."
5. major
6. minor. The narrator's brother is only mentioned briefly.
7. major. The narrator's father creates conflict in the story, and some of his life story is shared.
8. major. Mr. Butcher is the title character and central to the story's plot.
9. minor. Uncle Paul is mentioned in the story, but he is not central to the plot.
10. Answers should include something about Mr. Butcher being joyful and quick to laugh.
11. Answers should include his description "like a small dancing bear" and "a ready smile with eyes that crinkled when he laughed."
12. B.
13. A.
14. D.
15. D.
16. B.
17. introduction
18. climax
19. rising action
20. denouement
21. Sample answer: It's important for young people to pursue their dreams even if those dreams are not what the parents expect.

Unit 2: Reading Poetry and Drama

Lesson 1: Meter and Rhyme in Poetry

1. A division in a poem
2. The pattern of stressed and unstressed syllables in a line of poetry
3. Words that have the same vowel sound
4. B.
5. D.
6. C.

Lesson 2: Symbolism in Poetry

1. B.
2. A.
3. D.
4. E.
5. C.
6. F.
7. Sample answer: The colors represent the speaker's mood changes. The gray color represents the gloomy day and reflects the speaker's sad mood. She has been crying. The pink sky and the rainbow reflect her change of heart. She is optimistic at the end.
8. a rainbow

Lesson 3: Figurative Language in Poetry

1. line 2
2. alliteration
3. line 3
4. a blue bird and a ballerina
5. line 1
6. The bluebird is given the human quality of dancing.
7. hyperbole

Lesson 4: Tone in Poetry

1. cherry blossoms; memories of home
2. warmth; laugh and sing; sweet souvenirs; all was right
3. nostalgic; loving
4. The author uses the phrase "sweet souvenirs" to describe memories of childhood. This shows that the speaker is remembering childhood fondly and feeling nostalgic.

Lesson 5: Theme in Poetry

1. The subject of a poem is what is being described or discussed in a poem. The theme is the underlying idea expressed or explored in the poem.
2. in a single word or a short phrase that describes an idea or lesson the poet wants to pass on to the reader
3. the narrator's memories of childhood
4. The narrator feels happy recalling the childhood memories.
5. home; childhood

Lesson 6: Stage Directions in Drama

1. This play takes place in a campground near a lake on a summer afternoon.
2. He empties the poles, spikes, and other parts onto the ground.
3. The stage directions describe the setting and what the characters are doing when the action begins.
4. fake tree stumps, backpacks, camping equipment, a tent that has not been put together

Lesson 7: Dialogue in Drama

1. Because he is an architect.
2. I'm an architect; Dad, you're so stubborn.
3. She is frustrated because he is not paying attention to her.
4. Mr. Warren
5. Mr. Warren is having a difficult time assembling the tent.

Unit Practice Test

1. A. The speaker says that grief is a "heavy load," or a burden.
2. B. The speaker is attributing human emotion and actions to the willow in the line "I'd watch our willow cry."
3. C.
4. B.
5. D. The word *hiss* sounds like the sound of hissing, so it is an example of onomatopoeia.
6. D. Because the speaker describes a lonely state of mind, a "great heaviness," and feelings of loneliness the overall tone is sad, despite the more hopeful tone at the end of the poem.
7. B. The poem is about the load of grief becoming lighter over time.
8. D.
9. B.
10. C.

Unit 3: Reading Nonfiction

Lesson 1: Types of Nonfiction

1. a text about a person's life written by someone other than the subject
2. a text written about specific periods of the author's life
3. the story of a person's life written by that person
4. a text that contains information about a product
5. an article that tells the author's opinion about a work of art
6. any text that contains real information about real people, places, or events

Lesson 2: Main Idea and Supporting Details

1. The most important set of human remains that tells the story of early North American life is the skeleton known as Kennewick Man.
2. He was stocky and muscular, about 5 feet 7 inches tall, weighed 160 pounds, and was right handed.
3. Examination of the Kennewick Man skeleton revealed details about who he was and how he lived.
4. The U.S. Army Corps of Engineers is involved in a number of infrastructure projects throughout the world.

Lesson 3: Text Structure

1. B.
2. A.
3. D.
4. C.

Lesson 4: Drawing Conclusions

1. C.
2. A.
3. C.
4. D.

Lesson 5: Purpose

1. D.
2. C.
3. B.
4. A.

Lesson 6: Summarizing

1. a brief statement or restatement of main points
2. a broad statement or principle
3. a rewording to clarify meaning
4. generalization
5. example
6. Possible answer: Several steps are involved in proofreading an essay.

Lesson 7: Understanding Vocabulary

1. the surrounding words in the sentence that are clues to the meaning of a word
2. the main part of a word
3. the short element that comes before the word
4. B.
5. D.
6. A.

Unit Practice Test

1. B.
2. C.
3. C. The main idea is that everyone is at risk of dehydration in hot weather, not just athletes.
4. D. The author says that an "increased intake of liquids" usually takes care of moderate dehydration.
5. B.
6. C.
7. A.
8. D.
9. A.
10. generalization
11. example
12. example
13. Possible answer: Drink extra fluids when taking part in outdoor activities to keep from suffering from dehydration in hot weather.
14. D. The paragraph describes Curie's life in the order that events occurred, so it is in chronological order.
15. B. "As an adult" indicates time passing and Curie's life stage at the time of she moved, so it provides a clue that the passage is in chronological order.
16. A. Phrases such as "groundbreaking work" suggest Curie was a brilliant scientist.
17. C. The paragraph shows Curie's discovery of radium led to the development of radiology and new medical treatments. The word "because" is a clue that this is a cause and effect paragraph.

18. **B.** The author presents the discovery of radium as a positive development; because of radium, researchers could "diagnose and treat new diseases."

19. **D.**

20. **A.** The words "like" and "similarly" shows that the paragraph is comparing the two scientists.

21. **D.**

22. **C.** The author says that only "18 leading scientists from Europe" were invited to the conference. This detail shows that Curie must have been a highly regarded scientist.

Unit 4: Grammar and Usage

Lesson 1: Parts of Speech

1. a word that names a person, a place, a thing, or an idea
2. a word that describes an action or a state of being
3. a word that describes a noun or makes it more specific
4. a word that describes a verb, an adjective, or another adverb
5. a word that joins two or more words or parts of a sentence
6. a word that shows the relationship between a noun and another word in a sentence
7. because, and, either, or
8. although, but
9. and, yet

Lesson 2: Sentence Structure

1. the actor of a sentence
2. the action of a sentence
3. a sentence with a subject and predicate
4. when items in a list have the same grammatical form
5. an incomplete sentence that is missing a subject or predicate
6. two or more sentences combined inappropriately
7. predicate
8. parallel structure
9. subject
10. fragment
11. run-on sentence

Lesson 3: Types of Sentences

1. a sentence consisting of an independent clause

2. a sentence consisting of two independent clauses
3. a sentence consisting of an independent clause and one or more dependent clauses
4. a sentence consisting of more than one independent clause and one or more dependent clauses
5. a sentence consisting of more than one independent clause, improperly punctuated
6. One option: I turned left, and I immediately saw my friend walking toward me.
7. One option: Travis, who was scared of the dark, slept all night in the cabin with the lights on.
8. One option: The explorers split up at the Mississippi River; one turned south, while the other turned north.
9. One option: Mr. Vazquez did not enjoy spending time at the mall, since he found the crowds overwhelming.

Lesson 4: Commas

1. a sentence that contains two or more independent clauses
2. a sentence that has one independent clause and at least one dependent clause
3. three or more items in a sentence that follow one after another
4. a group of words that can be omitted from a sentence without changing its meaning
5. After the rain stopped,
6. Possible answer: Before he went to the movies, he took his dog for a walk.
7. a small town in Arizona; The phrase is set off from the rest of the sentence with commas. When you read the sentence without the phrase, the meaning is still the same.

Lesson 5: Punctuation

1. a punctuation mark that is used to join independent clauses in a compound sentence
2. a punctuation mark that is used to introduce a list, an explanation, or a description
3. a punctuation mark used to make one word from two or more words or word parts
4. :

   ,

   ,

   .

5. The word groups on either side of the semicolon are independent clauses and are related to each other.

Lesson 6: Agreement

1. A.
2. B.
3. C.
4. D.

Lesson 7: Capitalization

1. a word that names a specific person, place, thing, or idea
2. a word that names a type of person, place, thing, or idea
3. The school is located in Dallas, Texas.
4. Dr. Anderson helped our friend David with his science homework.
5. Mr. Smith is going to Washington, D.C., next week to meet with Sen. Durbin.
6. Our teacher Mrs. Rodriguez traveled to Germany and France last year.

Lesson 8: Verbs

1. invited
2. saw
3. drove
4. will visit
5. eats
6. starts
7. A team of experts investigated the accident at the lab.

Lesson 9: Spelling

1. C.
2. proceed
3. immobile
4. argument
5. their
6. effect

Unit Practice Test

1. **B.** *Made* is an action word. It is what Kara did to dinner. Therefore, it is a verb.
2. **D.** *Stunningly* ends in -*ly* and describes the adjective delicious. Therefore, it is an adverb.
3. **C.** *After* describes a time relationship to work. Therefore, it is a preposition.
4. **A.** *Dinner* is a thing rather than an action or a description. Therefore, it is a noun.
5. **C.** *And* connects two equal ideas: her coat from the closet and her hat from the cupboard. Therefore, it is a conjunction.

ANSWER KEY

6. Complete

7. Complete

8. Incomplete

9. Sample answer: Boxes upon boxes were piled in stacks in the warehouse.

10. Sample answer: Hannah, along with her sister and older brother, had never seen a live eagle before.

11. Sample answer: Before we left the house, we made sure we had our tickets to the show.

12. Dependent. *When April's sister Maria decided to come on the trip* cannot stand alone as an independent sentence.

13. Dependent. *Even though she was not interested in camping* cannot stand alone as an independent sentence.

14. Independent. *April made sure Maria had a good time* can stand alone as an independent sentence.

15. Independent. *Maria agreed afterward that it had been fun* can stand alone as an independent sentence.

16. Complex. This sentence consists of one independent and one dependent clause, so it is a complex sentence.

17. Compound. This sentence consists of two independent clauses, so it is a compound sentence.

18. Simple. This sentence consists of one independent clause, so it is a simple sentence.

19. A.

20. Student answers will vary but should include a correctly used comma and subsequent coordinating conjunction.

21. B.

22. D.

23. A.

24. C.

25. Our class is gong on a field trip to Washington, D.C., to visit the Lincoln Memorial.

26. Juan and Michael interviewed Mr. Kristoff for their social studies project on Saturday.

27. decorated

28. brought

29. explained

30. has invited

31. achieve

32. C.

33. scariest

34. all ready

35. accept

Lesson 1: Topic Sentences

1. a sentence that identifies the main idea of a paragraph

2. Answers should reference the number of people involved the effort, Harriet Tubman, and the Underground Railroad.

3. Answers will vary but should reference the idea that prior to the Civil War, a massive effort was made to free slaves by bringing them safely out of slave-owning states.

Lesson 2: Supporting Details

1. details in a paragraph that explain, describe, or give reasons for its topic sentence

2. Answers will vary but should reference that after fighting a war in order to build a new nation characterized by liberty, people wanted to see their liberties secured.

3. Answers will vary but should reference that James Madison proposed the Bill of Rights to support some of these freedoms.

4. Answers will vary but should reference that ratification ensured more freedoms for some Americans.

5. Answers will vary but should reference that freedoms for an increasing number of Americans have been secured over time.

Lesson 3: Transitions

1. a word or phrase that connects words or ideas

2. C.

3. A.

4. B.

5. C.

Unit Practice Test

1. C. This sentence reflects the main idea of the paragraph.

2. Sample answer: Massive government spending, combined with the sacrifices and contributions of a nationwide war effort, provided the economic boost needed to finally end the Great Depression.

3. A. Because the paragraph is mainly about President Roosevelt's attempts to improve the economy before World War II, sentence A provides the most relevant supporting detail.

4. C. The two sentences show a cause and an effect, so "for that reason" is the most appropriate transition.

Lesson 1: Types of Essays

1. expository

2. persuasive

3. persuasive

4. expository

5. persuasive

6. expository

Lesson 2: Prewriting

1. chronological order

2. conclusion

3. logical order

4. brainstorming

5. audience

6. body

7. tone

Lesson 3: Writing the Rough Draft

1. a paragraph that makes one specific point and provides supporting details for that point

2. a paragraph that summarizes an essay

3. a paragraph that introduces the topic or purpose of an essay

4. a word or phrase that shows the relationship between sentences or paragraphs

5. formal

6. informal

7. informal

8. formal

Lesson 4: Revising and Proofreading

1. the final version of an essay; the version that will be submitted

2. checking an essay for errors in spelling, grammar, and logic

3. very informal spoken language

4. Sample answer: Jaime asked his friend how he was.

5. Sample answer: Yesterday, she studied the book thoroughly for clues to the mystery.

6. Sample answer: After their run, she said she was exhausted.

7. The dog appeared very aggressive.

Unit Practice Test

1. C. The writer is trying to convince others of the need for bike lanes, so this is a persuasive essay.

2. D. The phrase "increase the risk of accidents" expresses the writer's serious tone (in center circle).

3. B.

4. opposes

5. logical

6. keep drivers in their lanes, force cyclists to share fewer lanes (implied), fewer lanes will increase accidents, bike lanes keep bikers safe (in center circle)

7. prewriting, drafting, revising, proofreading

8. chronological order or order of sequence

9. Sample answer: doesn't understand how to find. The phrases *get* and *come up with* are both informal.

10. Sample answer: many people. The expression *lots of* and the word *folks* are both informal.

11. Sample answer: when one considers the situation. The pronoun *you* and the phrase *look at it* are both informal.

12. Sample answer: It seems clear. The contraction *it's* and the phrase *pretty obvious* are both informal.

13. Therefore. The second sentence draws a conclusion from the first, so therefore is an appropriate transition.

14. On the other hand. The second sentence introduces an opposing idea.

15. Similarly. The second sentence compares an idea from the first.

16. Otherwise. The second sentence draws a conclusion from the first.

17. Man, flipped out

18. blown away, awesome

19. in the bag, check this, up for grabs

20. arguement, completly. The correct spellings are *argument* and *completely*.

21. wierd, embarassed. The correct spellings are *weird* and *embarrassed*.

22. finaly, calender. The correct spellings are *finally* and *calendar*.

GLOSSARY

active voice — a verb form that emphasizes the subject doing the action

adjective — a word that describes a person, place, or thing

adverb — a word that describes a verb

agreement — when a verb and noun are consistent in number or gender

alliteration — the repetition of the same vowel or consonant sound in several words

antecedent — the subject to which a pronoun refers

author's purpose — the reason an author writes a text

autobiography — a story a person writes about his or her own life

biography — a story about a person's life written by someone other than the subject

body — the middle of an essay

body paragraph — a paragraph in the body of an essay

brainstorming — freely thinking about a number of ideas

cause and effect — a text structure that explains why something happened or describes the effects of an event

character — a person or role within a story

characterization — the way in which a character's traits are described

chronological order — a text structure that tells a sequence of events in time order or as ordered steps in a process

climax — the turning point of a story

colon — a punctuation mark used to introduce a list of items

comma — a punctuation mark used to separate words and phrases in a sentence

common noun — a type of person, place, thing, or idea

compare and contrast — a text structure that describes similarities and/or differences of two or more things

complete sentence — a sentence that contains a subject and predicate and expresses a complete thought

complex sentence — a sentence with at least one independent and one dependent clause

compound sentence — a sentence with two independent clauses joined by a coordinating conjunction

compound-complex sentence — a sentence that contains more than one independent clause and at least one dependent clause

conclusion — the end of an essay

conflict — the problem that occurs when two opposing forces meet

conjunction — a word that connects two or more words or groups of words

connotation — the impression a word leaves on a reader

coordinating conjunction — a word that links two independent clauses

dash — a punctuation mark that demonstrates a break in thought

declarative sentence — a statement

denotation — the literal meaning of a word

denouement — the conclusion of a story

dependent clause — a clause with a noun and verb that is not a complete sentence

description — text that describes features and characteristics of a person, object, or place

dialogue — a conversation that takes place between two characters

direct characterization — a narrator's description of a character's traits

direct tone — a tone in which the writer's attitude is clearly stated

drama — a written work intended to be performed by actors

draw a conclusion — to form a judgment after reading all of a text

end rhyme — a rhyme that appears at the end of a line of poetry

essay — a nonfiction text that describes, explains, or analyzes a topic

example — a specific detail that explains or supports a generalization

exclamation — a statement that exclaims something

exclamation point — a punctuation mark used at the end of an exclamation

explain — to give instructions or to teach the reader how to do something

explanatory — explaining something about a topic

expository essay — a text that provides information or explains something

external conflict — a conflict between one character and another, or between a character and an outside force

falling action — the events that occur after the climax and conclude the story

figure of speech — a phrase used in a nonliteral sense, such as a simile or metaphor

final draft — the last version of an essay

first-person — a point of view in which the story is happening to the narrator

formal — professional, sophisticated

fragment — an incomplete sentence

generalization — a broad statement or main idea

grammar — the way words fit together to form sentences

homonyms — words that are pronounced the same way but have different meanings and spellings

hyperbole — an exaggeration

hyphen — a punctuation mark used to join compound words

idiom — a phrase that has a fixed meaning

implied tone — a tone in which the writer's attitude is not stated directly

independent clause — a clause with a noun and verb that can stand alone as a complete sentence

indirect characterization — characterization that must be inferred through a character's words or actions, or through the author's tone

inference — an assumption based on logic and the text

inform — to provide facts about people, places, or ideas

informal — casual

informative — providing facts about a topic

internal conflict — a conflict that occurs within a character's inner self

internal rhyme — a rhyme that appears in the middle of a line of poetry

interrogative sentence — a question

introduction — the beginning of an essay

introductory phrase — a phrase that provides additional information about the main part of a sentence

irregular verbs — verbs that form their past tense in a way other than adding -d or -ed to the base form

main idea — the most important idea in a piece of writing

major character — an important character in a story

memoir — a text written about short periods of the author's life

metaphor — a comparison of two unlike things with no connecting word

meter — the pattern of the rhythm of stressed and unstressed syllables

minor character — a less important or supporting character in a story

mood — the atmosphere or feeling in a work of fiction

narrator — the person telling the story

near rhyme — the repetition of similar sounds

nonfiction — any text that contains real information about real people, places, or events

nonfiction prose — text that contains facts

nonrestrictive phrase — a phrase that is not essential to a sentence's meaning

noun — a person, place, or thing

number — the singular or plural form of a noun or verb

onomatopoeia — a word that imitates or suggests the sound of the thing itself

parallel structure — a list format in which items are in the same form

paraphrase — a shorter, reworded version of a longer text

passive voice — a verb form that shifts the emphasis from who or what performed the action to the action itself

period — a punctuation mark used at the end of a sentence

personification — a literary device that gives human attributes and emotions to nonliving things

persuade — to convince the reader to agree with the writer's opinion

persuasive essay — a text that provides an opinion or tries to convince the reader to do or believe something

phonetically — according to the sounds

play — a drama performed on a stage

plot — the events that take place in a story, including the introduction, rising action, climax, falling action, and denouement

plural — referring to more than one person or thing

GLOSSARY

point of view — the perspective of the person telling the story

predicate — the part of a sentence that contains a verb and tells what the subject does or is

prefix — a short element that comes before the root of a word

preposition — a word that shows the relationship between a noun and another part of a sentence

prewriting — the first step in writing, during which ideas are formed

prior knowledge — knowledge that is learned from previous experience or study

problem and solution — a text structure that states a problem and offers a solution

pronoun — a word that can replace a noun in a sentence

proofread — to read carefully to check for errors

proper noun — a specific person, place, thing, or idea

question mark — a punctuation mark used at the end of a question

regular verbs — verbs whose past tense is formed by adding -d or -ed to the base form

review — an article that tells the author's opinion about something

revise — to rewrite a draft of an essay to improve it

rhyme — the repetition of the same vowel sound

rhyme scheme — a pattern of rhymes

rhythm — the pattern of stressed and unstressed syllables in a poem

rising action — the main body of the story, which leads up to the climax

root — the base or main part of a word

run-on sentence — two or more independent clauses that are not connected with correct punctuation

semicolon — a punctuation mark that connects two thoughts in one sentence

series — a list of three or more items

setting — the time and place in which a story takes place

simile — a comparison of two unlike things linked by a connecting word, such as *like* or *as*

simple sentence — the most basic type of sentence, made up of one independent clause

singular — referring to one person or thing

slang — very informal language

stage directions — the instructions the author uses to guide the players in a drama

stanza — a division in a poem that consists of two or more (but usually four) lines

subject — the person, place, thing, or idea performing the action in a sentence

suffix — a short element that comes after the root of a word

summary — a brief statement or restatement of main points

supporting detail — a detail found in the body of a paragraph that supports the main idea

syllable — a word part with one sound

symbol — a person, place, thing, or event in a work of literature that represents something else

tense — the form of a verb that indicates when the action or state of being takes place

text features — features, such as headings or subheadings, that make nonfiction text easier to read

text structure — the organization of a text

theme — the main idea in a work of literature

third-person — a point of view in which the story is happening to a character other than the narrator

third-person limited — a point of view from which the narrator can describe the thoughts and feelings of only one character

third-person omniscient — a point of view from which the narrator can describe the thoughts and feelings of multiple characters

tone — the attitude of the writer toward the characters or events in a work of literature

topic sentence — a sentence that includes the main idea and/or topic of a piece of writing

transition — a word or phrase used to connect ideas in sentences and paragraphs

usage — the traditions governing how speakers and writers use a language

user manual — a text that contains information about or instructions for using a product

verb — a word that expresses action or a state of being

verbal context — the words and sentences surrounding a word